Asia:
Its Growth and Agony

Toshio Watanabe

An East-West Center Book

Institute for

Economic Development and Policy

© 1992 by the East-West Center

Manufactured in the United States of America

Library of Congress Cataloging-in-Publication Data

Watanabe, Toshio, 1939–
  [Ajia keizai o dō toraeru ka. English]
  Asia, its growth and agony / Toshio Watanabe.
     p.   cm.
  Includes index.
  ISBN 0–86638–143–0 : $16.00
  1. Asia—Economic conditions—1945– I. Title.
HC412.W361313   1992
338.95—dc20   91–22946
                                                    CIP

The original Japanese version of this book,
Ajia Keizai o dō Toraeru ka, was published
in 1991 by Nippon Hoso Shuppan Kyokai.

Distributed by the University of Hawaii Press
2840 Kolowalu Street, Honolulu, Hawaii 96822

CONTENTS

LIST OF FIGURES

LIST OF TABLES

PREFACE

Asia is huge and diversified. It comprises countries that span from South Asia, where the majority of people live in absolute poverty, to the Asian NIEs (newly industrializing economies) where people live in the midst of the mass consumption era. Bangladesh, which suffers from extreme poverty, and South Korea, which competes intensely with developed countries in the area of high-tech products, are both countries in Asia.

Because it is not easy to provide a single analytical framework which can uniformly grasp the economies of this diversified region, a unique methodological approach was adopted in this book. Countries in Asia have been divided into four economically similar groups, namely, South Asia, Southeast Asia, the Asian NIEs, and China. The following issues concerning the development of each group have been tackled:

1. What is the cause of extreme poverty in the countries of South Asia?
2. Is Southeast Asia really experiencing genuine economic modernization?
3. How did the Asian NIEs take off from the stage of underdevelopment to become leading industrial economies?
4. Where is the bold economic reform leading China?

It is extraordinarily difficult to answer these questions. Nevertheless, being fully aware of this difficulty, it is my intent to express my views rather freely and resolutely in this book. There is no firmly established theory for the interpretation of the issues relating to development. Rather this book is meant to offer my personal views, and I would be pleased to find that this book serves to provide the reader that is contemplating the problems of Asia with some ideas.

The original Japanese version of this book was completed with the refining of the textbook used for the NHK's Citizens College Lecture Series "Asia: Its Growth and Agony" which was televised in Japan during April–June 1988. During the series, I had the experience of speaking to an unseen audience of millions. The magnitude of the audience was beyond the imagination of a person like me who does research in a university study room. I tried to cover a wide range of topics without going into too much detail and I attempted to communicate with the audience using language that was as plain as possible. This book was prepared in the same way.

Because there are few introductory books on the economies of contemporary Asia, this book is a useful contribution. This book was meant to be used in classrooms and seminars as educational material. Hence, a number of tables and graphs were used to incorporate as much information as possible. Because it was intended as an introductory guidebook, the book does not contain detailed notes on references. However, readers who are interested in looking further into a subject should directly refer to the excellent sources of the tables and graphs.

This book was originally written for Japanese readers, particularly students. However, in view of its favorable reception in Japan, my old friends currently working in the Asian Development Bank (ADB) suggested that an English version of the book would be of great value to other students who are interested in the development of Asia. I am honored and happy to see my book translated into English and to know that it will be available to more people. I am, therefore, greatly indebted to Messrs. Tsuneaki Yoshida, Hiroshi Kakazu, Masahiro Otsuka, Kazu Sakai, and Ayumi Konishi of ADB for the translation and their comments. Thanks are also extended to Mr. Graham Colin-Jones of ADB and Ms. Janis Togashi of East-West Center for their comments and endeavors in the English editing.

Toshio Watanabe
December 1991

CHAPTER ONE

Race Against Population Growth

Excess Population in Asia

Many Asian countries have long been suffering from the "excessive" size of their populations and the high rate of population growth. South Asian countries such as Bangladesh, India, and Pakistan are particularly well-known for their population-related problems. But the situation in certain Southeast Asian countries such as the Philippines and Indonesia is no better than that in South Asia. They are all facing the problem of "excess" population.

A country can be said to have excess population in relation to the availability of cultivated land. While these Asian countries have already almost exhausted their undeveloped cultivable land, their population is still growing at a high rate. As a consequence, cultivated land per capita in these countries has been steadily decreasing.

Until recently, Thailand and Myanmar (Burma) were regarded as being sufficiently endowed, in relation to the size of their population, with rich, fertile land that is suitable for growing rice. However, even in these countries, their undeveloped land resources are reaching the point of complete depletion following continuous massive population growth. Figure 1.1 illustrates the changes in cultivated land area per capita in these Asian countries during the 1970s. The land area that was available to each farmer in 1970 was very limited, and by the end of the decade, the situation had worsened.

Since cultivable land has become scarce, the introduction of new agricultural technology is now an urgent task. Land productivity (yield per unit area) must be increased in order to utilize available land more effectively. Responding to this need, the Green Revolution took place in Asia during the 1970s. Hybrid seeds or high-yield varieties (HYVs) of rice were gradually introduced to Asian farmers to replace the traditional varieties that were characterized by low productivity. (The details of the Green Revolution will be discussed further in Chapter 3.)

Nevertheless, the improvement in land productivity brought about by the introduction of new technology, or the Green Revolution, has not been sufficient to overtake the growth in population. Per capita production (labor productivity) has been stagnant or even decreasing in some countries

1

Figure 1.1 PER CAPITA CULTIVATED LAND IN SELECTED ASIAN COUNTRIES

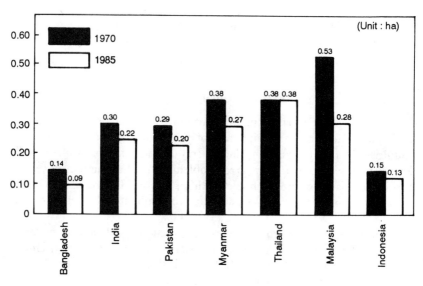

SOURCE :   Food and Agriculture Organization. *Production Yearbook*. Rome: FAO.

Table 1.1
Indicators of Nutrition in Selected Asian Countries

COUNTRY	FOOD (1979–1981 = 100)		CALORIE (CALORIE)		PROTEIN (GRAMS)	
	1965	1985	1965	1985	1965	1985
Bangladesh	105	98	1,960	1,870	41	41
India	101	110	2,150	2,180	55	53
Pakistan	96	101	2,190	2,180	59	56
South Korea			2,280	2,810	59	78

SOURCES: Food and Agriculture Organization. *Production Yearbook*. Rome: FAO; ADB. *Key Indicators of Developing Member Countries of ADB*. Manila: ADB.

because of the persistent massive population growth. Given this situation, it is not easy to raise the income level of farmers. The situation has been particularly serious in South Asian countries. As can be seen in Table 1.1, in the last ten years per capita food production increased by less than 10 percent in India, 5 percent in Pakistan, and in Bangladesh it has even decreased. The table also indicates that the daily calorie intake per person in Bangladesh and Pakistan also decreased, and the protein intake per person per day barely remained constant or decreased in these three countries. The development problems caused by population growth will be discussed throughout this book.

Even today, the rate of population growth in many Asian countries is extremely high. These rates are far higher than the maximum rates ever experienced by the developed countries in the past. Table 1.2 indicates the maximum annual population growth rates experienced by the developed countries as estimated by Professor Simon Kuznets. Apart from the United States where high population growth due to immigration was recorded, Russia (USSR) and the Netherlands experienced the fastest population growth among the developed countries where the rates reached 1.5 and 1.4 percent, respectively, during the period from the late 18th century to the first three decades of the 20th century. In other developed countries, the peak rates were only a little above 1 percent.

As can be seen from Table 1.3, which shows the annual population growth rates of Asian countries during the recent census periods, the rate of population growth in the Asian countries today is more than twice that experienced by the developed countries in the past. In Pakistan, the population has been increasing at a rate of 3.1 percent per annum, and in Malaysia and in the Philippines, the growth rate is 2.8 percent. The dreadful implication of these figures may be better understood from the fact that if a country's population continues to increase at a rate of 3.1 percent per annum, the population of that country will double in only 23 years. A rate of 2.8 percent means a doubling time of 26 years.

Table 1.2
Peak Population Growth Rates Recorded in Developed Countries

COUNTRY	PERIOD	PEAK POPULATION GROWTH RATE (%)
France	1831/40–1861/70	0.4
Germany	1925/29–1950/54	1.2
Italy	1925/29–1951/54	0.7
Japan	1904–1938	1.3
Netherlands	1890/1900–1925/29	1.4
Sweden	1885/94–1905/14	0.7
United Kingdom	1801/11–1851/61/71	1.3
United States	1834/43–1859	3.1
USSR	1870–1913	1.5

SOURCE: Kuznets, S. 1971. *Economic Growth of Nations*. Cambridge: Harvard University Press.

Table 1.3
Population Growth in Asia (percentage)

COUNTRY	PERIOD	POPULATION GROWTH RATE
Bangladesh	1974–1981	2.4
India	1971–1981	2.3
Indonesia	1971–1980	2.3
Malaysia	1970–1980	2.8
Myanmar (Burma)	1973–1983	2.2
Pakistan	1972–1981	3.1
Philippines	1975–1980	2.8
Singapore	1970–1980	1.5
South Korea	1980–1985	1.5
Thailand	1970–1980	2.5

SOURCES: Country censuses.

The Demographic Transition

What has caused this rapid population growth in the Asian countries? In order to consider this problem, the theory of the "demographic transition" should first be discussed. This empirical law explains why and how modern developed nations have passed through more or less similar historical "stages" of population trends in relation to their economic development. To provide a conceptual framework for this law of demographic transition, Figure 1.2 illustrates the relationship between the birth rate, the death rate, and the rate of population growth (the difference between the birth rate and the death rate) using time-series data. The vertical axis indicates the changes in these rates and the horizontal axis indicates the time flow.

A historical examination of the population movements in many countries indicates that a country's population typically passes through four stages over the course of modernization. These stages are: (1) very stable or slowly growing population as a result of the combination of a high birth rate and an almost equally high death rate (Stage I); (2) a rapid population increase as a result of a continued high birth rate or only a beginning of its gradual decline combined with a drastic decline in the death rate resulting from modernization (Stage II); (3) an eventual slowing down in the pace of decline in the death rate and an acceleration of the decline in the birth date resulting in a contraction of the population growth rate (Stage III); and (4) the society's entry into another stable situation with little or no population growth resulting from a further decline in the birth rate until it reaches or almost reaches the same level as the death rate which declined earlier (Stage IV). Through this process, a country's population growth rate in the long

Figure 1.2 DEMOGRAPHIC TRANSITION

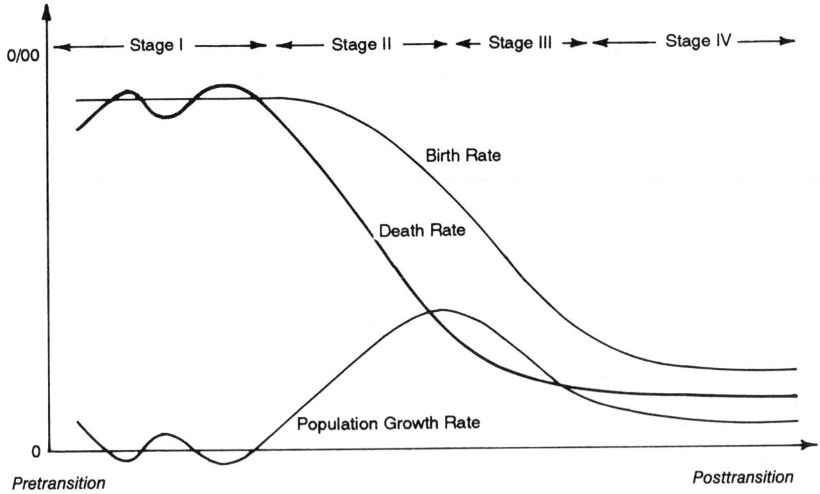

run increases from a very low level to a high level, and then returns to a low level along its development path. This pattern or the "demographic transition" has been observed in many countries and it is considered to be a highly plausible hypothesis.

During the period of premodernization or at an early stage of development which is on the left of Figure 1.2 (Stage I), a large portion of a country's population generally suffers from poverty and its death rate is high. Accordingly, a society at this stage has to have a high birth rate that is at least sufficient to offset the high death rate in order for the society to maintain its size and to survive. Therefore, the social norms, customs, and system of such a society are formed to foster a high birth rate. A poor society usually has an extremely high birth rate because its death rate is high. Empirically, this tendency appears to exist in most of the countries as Figures 1.3 and 1.4 indicate the strong positive correlation between the infant mortality rate (the ratio of infants who die before reaching one year of age) and the birth rate, and the strong negative correlation between the life expectancy at birth and the birth rate.

The death rate begins to decrease when modernization brings to a society economic development which is accompanied by better diets, provision of clean water and a sewerage system, improved health facilities, and programs such as group inoculation schemes against smallpox, to name just a few. However, a decline in the death rate is not usually followed immediately by a decline in the birth rate as the society's norms or culture which supported the high birth rate cannot be adjusted overnight. The birth rate tends to

Figure 1.3 CORRELATION BETWEEN INFANT MORTALITY RATES AND BIRTH RATES IN ASIA, 1982

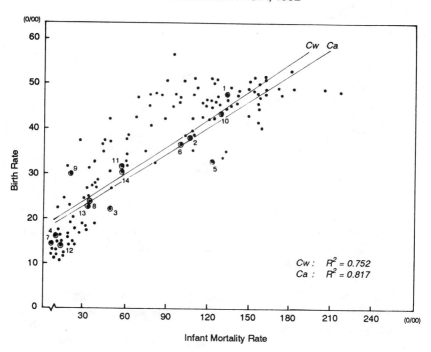

NOTES :
    Cw: Regression based on the worldwide statistics
    Ca: Regression based on the statistics of Asian countries

COUNTRIES :
    1   Bangladesh
    2   Myanmar (Burma)
    3   China
    4   Hong Kong
    5   India
    6   Indonesia
    7   Japan
    8   South Korea
    9   Malaysia
   10 Pakistan
   11 Philippines
   12 Singapore
   13 Sri Lanka
   14 Thailand

SOURCE :   United Nations. *Demographic Yearbook.* New York: UN.

Figure 1.4 CORRELATION BETWEEN LIFE EXPECTANCY AT BIRTH AND BIRTH RATES IN ASIA, 1982

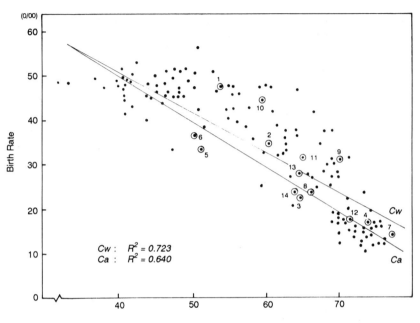

Cw : $R^2 = 0.723$
Ca : $R^2 = 0.640$

Average Life Expectancy at Birth (years)

NOTES :   Cw: Regression based on the worldwide statistics
            Ca: Regression based on the statistics of Asian countries

COUNTRIES :   1   Bangladesh
              2   Myanmar (Burma)
              3   China
              4   Hong Kong
              5   India
              6   Indonesia
              7   Japan
              8   South Korea
              9   Malaysia
              10 Pakistan
              11 Philippines
              12 Singapore
              13 Sri Lanka
              14 Thailand

SOURCE :   United Nations. *Demographic Yearbook.* New York: UN.

remain at a high level for some time after the death rate starts declining. As a result, the growing difference between a continuing high birth rate and a falling death rate leads to a sharp increase in the population growth rate. Stage II thus marks the beginning of the demographic transition, i.e., a transition from the initial condition of a stable or slowly growing population to a period in which the society's population increases rapidly. Then in Stage III, the birth rate declines rapidly while the death rate reaches a lower level and becomes stable. Thus, during this stage there will be a decline in the population growth rate. Eventually, the falling birth rate converges with the lower death rate; as a result, there will be little or no population growth and the situation will again become stable. The mechanism through which the birth rate declines during Stage III will be examined in the next chapter.

This process of change in population growth was first experienced in the United Kingdom (i.e., England and Wales) and then in other Western European countries, Japan, and Russia (Figure 1.5). For example, in the United Kingdom where consistent demographic statistics have been maintained the longest, the birth rate was constantly high at around 35 per mil

Figure 1.5 DEMOGRAPHIC TRENDS: UNITED KINGDOM (ENGLAND AND WALES), JAPAN AND INDIA

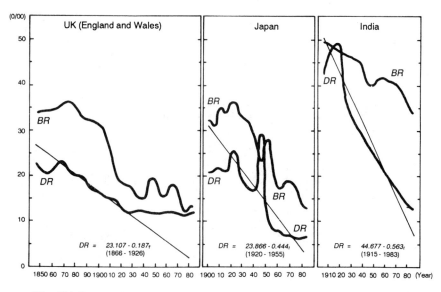

BR : Birth Rate
DR : Death Rate

SOURCES :   B. R. Mitchell. 1982. *International Historical Statistics*. London: Macmillan Press;
United Nations. *Demographic Yearbook*. New York: UN.

(1/1000) from the mid-18th century until about 1880 when it started to decline. In contrast, the death rate began to decline gradually from the mid-18th century (not shown in the figure), then stabilized somewhat in the early 19th century, and then began to decline again in the 1870s.

The population growth rate in the United Kingdom therefore increased rapidly from the mid-18th century and reached its peak of 15 to 16 per mil between 1870 and 1880. After this period, however, the birth rate declined much faster than the death rate; this situation continued until about 1940. The death rate stabilized at a low level in 1930 when the birth rate was still decreasing. As a result, the population growth rate in the United Kingdom reached its peak in the 1870s and then constantly declined until the beginning of World War II. In the postwar period, the population growth rate has been generally constant at a low level with occasional minor fluctuations. A similar demographic transition can be observed in Japan with the exception of the irregularities associated with World War II.

In order to observe the demographic transition process in today's Asian countries, let us take India as an example. At the beginning of this century, the birth rate in India was extremely high at around 50 per mil, and the death rate, though fluctuating due to periodic famines and epidemics, always remained above 40 per mil (except for a few years). This high birth rate has continued until very recently; it fell below 40 per mil (to the range of 30–40 per mil) only in the 1970s. Presently, the birth rate in India is estimated to be as high as 34 per mil. On the other hand, the death rate started to decline much earlier and fell below 40 per mil in the 1920s, was 20–30 per mil after World War II, and was 10–20 per mil in the mid-1960s. Today, the death rate has reached a low level of 11 per mil. As a combination of these two movements, the population growth rate in India started to increase in the 1920s and continued to accelerate to reach the present high rate of 23 per mil.

It should be noted that the demographic transition in today's Asian countries, as compared to that of the developed countries, has some peculiar characteristics. First, the initial death rates in the Asian countries were much higher than that of the developed countries in the premodernization period, and consequently, the initial birth rates were also higher. Second, the death rates have declined much faster in the Asian countries while the adjustments in the birth rates have not occurred at the same pace. From Figure 1.5, it is clear that the initial death rate in India was much higher than that of the United Kingdom and Japan; and the period required for the death rate to reach a lower stable level was rather long in the case of the United Kingdom, was shorter in Japan, and was much shorter in India. In other words, the pace of reduction in the death rate was far more rapid in India as compared to the other two countries while the birth rate has been declining only very gradually.

Population Growth and Economic Development

Apart from its size and speed, the reduction in death rates in Asia is different from that of the developed countries in terms of its background and its cause. Through the process of development, the economic growth or increase in income level in the developed countries "internally" induced the reduction in the death rate. In the Western European countries and Japan, an increase in industrial productivity resulting from the Industrial Revolution took place concurrently with the reduction in their death rates, and in the case of Western Europe, the Agricultural Revolution even preceded the Industrial Revolution. In Japan, both revolutions took place almost simultaneously. The increase in agricultural and industrial output and the consequent increase in income resulted in an improvement in people's diet, in living standards, and in social infrastructure such as the transportation system and medical facilities. These also contributed to the advancement of medical knowledge and technology as well as to the people's improved awareness of the importance of hygiene. In other words, economic development provided society with the basic conditions or prerequisites for the reduction of the death rate. In this sense, the causes of the reduction in the death rate in the Western European countries and Japan more or less originated from "internal" or endogenous factors.

On the contrary, the reduction of death rates in the Asian countries are various "external" or exogenous factors. For example, during colonial days, the developed countries introduced law and order to Asian societies in order to facilitate administration of territories and to ensure the security of those administering the territories. This, in turn, resulted in a reduction of casualties from tribal conflicts. In addition, transportation and communication networks developed by the colonial governments facilitated relief activities in rural areas in the case of famines and this also contributed substantially towards the reduction in death rates. But most notable and important is modern medical technology that was provided to the Asian countries after World War II for the prevention of epidemics and which had a dramatic impact.

In Sri Lanka, for example, malaria was the most significant cause of the high death rate of over 40 per mil until 1940. In the early 1940s, a large-scale sprinkling of an insecticide known as DDT (dichloro diphenyle tricholoro ethane) over marsh areas almost completely exterminated the malarial mosquitoes in the country. As a result, following the introduction of DDT, the death rate decreased to 14 per mil in 1947, 10 per mil in 1954, and 8 per mil in as early as 1972. This was the lowest death rate this country had ever experienced. As a result, the population growth rate in Sri Lanka increased from 17 per mil in the early 1940s, to 25 per mil in 1947, and then to 27 per mil in

1954. This high rate has been maintained since. A study attributes 42 percent of the reduction in the death rate between 1946 and 1960 to the extermination of malarial mosquitoes by DDT.

In Asian countries, many fatal epidemics such as malaria, yellow fever, smallpox, and cholera were brought under control only after World War II. Medications, such as antibiotics, sulphur drugs, and vaccines, and insecticides such as DDT, that had been developed by and that were widely used in the developed countries were introduced to the Asian countries at very low prices, or at no cost, through foreign assistance after World War II. This is considered to be the most important factor behind the drastic reduction in death rates in Asia. In addition, after these colonies obtained their independence, the new governments undertook many large-scale programs and policies for the improvement of public health through the provision of better medical facilities and through various projects that were targeted for the masses. Many new hospitals and clinics were built to greatly increase people's accessibility to these facilities. This improvement in the field of public health was of extreme importance and can be viewed as almost "revolutionary" for these countries.

Reduction in infant mortality rates have contributed considerably to the reduction in death rates. As shown in Table 1.4, there were significant declines in infant mortality (0 to 1 year of age) and child death rates (1 to 4 years of age) between 1965 and 1985. External impacts have caused a drastic population increase in Asian countries which did not have internal socioeconomic conditions or prerequisites for a decline in death rates. In other

Table 1.4
Infant Mortality and Child Death Rates in Selected Asian Countries
(per mil)

	INFANT MORTALITY RATE (0–1 YEAR OLD)		CHILD DEATH RATE (1–4 YEARS OLD)	
	1965	1985	1965	1985
Bangladesh	153	125	24	18
India	151	89	23	11
Indonesia	138	96	20	12
Malaysia	55	28	5	2
Myanmar (Burma)	122	66	21	na
Pakistan	149	115	23	16
Philippines	72	48	21	11
Thailand	88	43	11	3

NOTE: na = not available.
SOURCE: United Nations. *Demographic Yearbook*. New York: UN.

words, rapid population growth has taken place in Asian countries despite the fact that the socioeconomic prerequisites for an internally induced reduction in death rates did not exist, because there were many external forces that were aimed directly at reducing the death rate.

It is easy to imagine that an explosive population growth which takes place prior to or independently from a country's socioeconomic development poses an extremely heavy burden on the country's future economic development. If a country's population increases along with its economic growth, the growth in population can contribute positively to the country's development since population is the source of labor supply which, in turn, is required for production. Moreover, a country's population constitutes a market that generates demand for the economy's output. However, in many Asian countries, a "population explosion" or a massive increase in population occurred without being accompanied by economic development. In this situation, increased population can only result in the accumulation of excess labor.

In addition, a high birth rate implies that a country's population is becoming more youthful as more children are added. This means that the relative size of the dependent population which must be supported by economically active adults (i.e., the independent population) becomes larger. A typical population pyramid of a country with a high birth rate is one which has a relatively large base (Figure 1.6A). A country with a low birth rate has a population pyramid similar to Figure 1.6B. If we consider those below 15 years of age as youthful dependents and those between 15 and 64 years of age as the independent population, the ratio of these two, i.e., the youth dependency ratio, presents the number of youthful dependents each member of the labor force must support. A high youth dependency ratio poses a heavy burden on a country's economy as a whole as well as on its labor force since the economy will be required to allocate more resources to education, public health, and the consumption of people who do not contribute to production; hence, less resources will be available for investment and production. As indicated in Figure 1.7, the dependency burden, as expressed by the youth dependency ratio, in the Asian countries is notably higher than those of the Asian Newly Industrializing Economies (NIEs: Hong Kong, South Korea, Singapore, and Taiwan) and the developed countries.

Given this situation, many Asian countries have been forced to reduce their already low savings and even less resources are available for investment to increase future production. Thus, population growth has caught many Asian countries in a vicious circle from which it is extremely difficult to escape despite their efforts and desire for socioeconomic development.

Figure 1.6 POPULATION PYRAMIDS OF THE PHILIPPINES AND THE UNITED KINGDOM

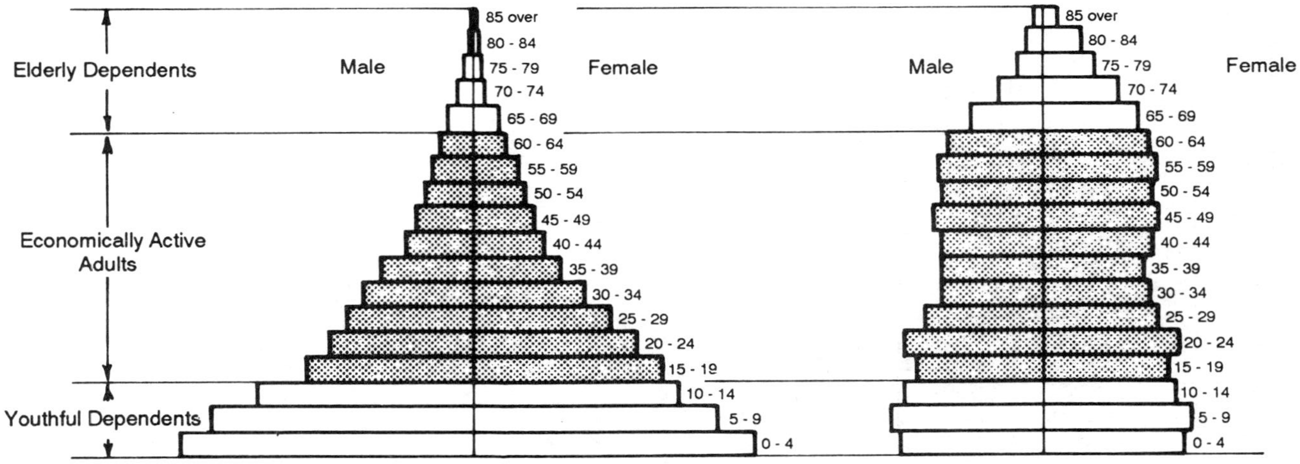

PHILIPPINES
(A)

UNITED KINGDOM
(B)

Figure 1.7 YOUTH DEPENDENCY RATIO IN SELECTED COUNTRIES, 1985*

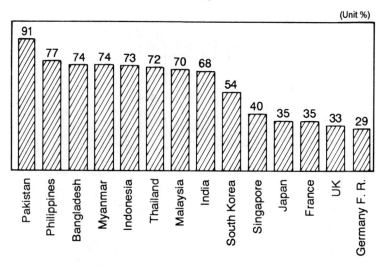

(Unit %)

NOTE :   *(Youth Dependency Ratio) = (Youth Dependents)/(Economically Active Adults).

SOURCE :   United Nations. *Demographic Yearbook.* New York: UN.

CHAPTER TWO

Economic Development and Birth Rate

Economics of Childbearing

Is it possible to predict how the present situation of "excess" population in Asia will develop? In other words, is it reasonable to expect to see the final stage of the demographic transition process in the Asian countries as was the case of the developed countries? Since the death rates in many countries have already declined to a minimal level, the question is whether there is any hope that the birth rates will be significantly reduced. In order to answer this question, it may be useful to examine the socioeconomic environment, as it affects childbearing, in developed countries where the birth rates have reached a stable, low level.

It is reasonable to state that economic development accompanies a decline in death rates. In any age and in any society, it is quite normal for one to desire a healthy long life; in fact, it is human nature to do so. If there is an opportunity to lower the death rate through an increase in income level, people will immediately attempt to take advantage of the chance. Given that we accept the existence of human instinct for survival, it is logical to assume a clear relationship between economic development and the movement of death rates.

On the other hand, the relationship between economic development and birth rates is not as clear. In order for a poor society with a high death rate to maintain its existence, it is essential for the society to also sustain a high birth rate. For this reason, custom or a social norm that values a high birth rate was widely accepted. Since the custom or social norm to sustain high birth rates was established over a long period of time, it cannot be altered easily even with dramatic declines in death rates. If the people's attitude towards childbearing is influenced by the religion of the society, it is even more difficult to change the situation. Nevertheless, in all of the developed countries, birth rates eventually declined after the fall in the death rates though with some time lag.

Data show that countries with low income levels tend to have higher birth rates while countries with higher income levels have lower birth rates (Figure 2.1). Moreover, empirical analyses indicate that in a poor society, parents tend to have many children, and as the society becomes wealthier, the number of children born per family in that society decreases. How and why could

Figure 2.1 CORRELATION BETWEEN BIRTH RATES AND PER CAPITA INCOME, 1985

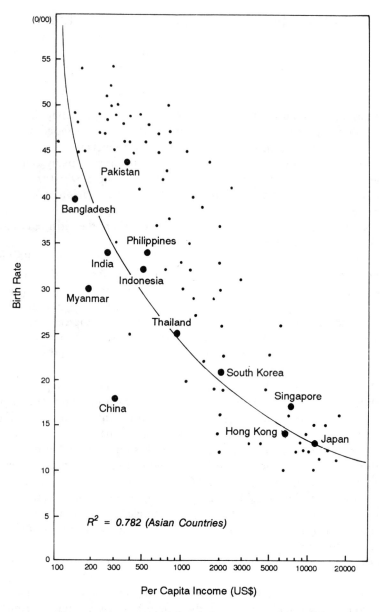

SOURCE : World Bank. 1987. *World Development Report.* New York: WB.

this happen? The explanation provided by population economics is given in the following paragraphs.

When parents consider whether they should have an additional child, they must compare the utility and disutility of having the child. If the utility is larger than the disutility, they choose to have the additional child and if it is not, they decide otherwise. What then are the factors concerning the utility and disutility of having children?

Three factors have been considered to affect the utility of having children. The first factor is genuine "instinct." By human nature, people are normally pleased to have and raise children with love and care. This instinctive satisfaction arising from simply being parents comprises an important part of the utility. The second factor is "income." In a poor society, children often become very important contributors to family income by being fully active working members of families. The third factor is "welfare" or "social security." In many poor societies, having children is often the only way for parents to safeguard their well-being in old age in the absence of any reliable social welfare system.

On the other hand, two factors contribute to the disutility of having children. First, there is a direct cost involved in raising children as parents have to feed them, provide them with shelter and clothing, send them to school, etc. There is also an "indirect cost" or an "opportunity cost" involved as parents, especially mothers, must forego opportunities to work and earn income if they are to bear and raise children.

What then happens to the utility and disutility of having children as a country's economy develops and per capita income increases? Let us first consider the factors that affect utility.

The first factor, instinct, would not be affected by economic development. Regardless of the income level of a society, parents would by human nature love their children. For this reason, the relationship between the per capita income level (horizontal axis) and the utility level of this factor (A ') is shown to be constant in Figure 2.2.

What about the income factor? As the economy develops, child labor would be replaced by formally employed workers. In addition, an increase in income level would reduce the dependency of the household budget on children's contribution to family income; therefore, there would also be less necessity for children to work. Children would further lose opportunities to work since imposition of compulsory education and legislation prohibiting or restricting child labor would make it difficult. Furthermore, economic development itself would raise the skill levels required by the job market. Accordingly, in Figure 2.2, the utility of the income factor (B ') is expressed by a downward slope.

With regard to the welfare or social security factor, it would not be hard to

Figure 2.2 UTILITY AND DISUTILITY OF HAVING AN ADDITIONAL CHILD (I)

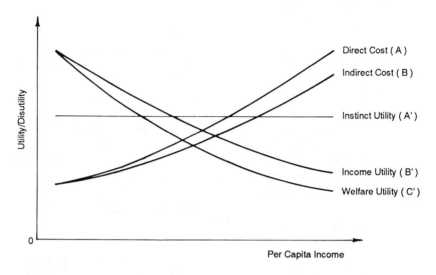

imagine that parents would depend less on their children for support as they become older if their income level increases and there exists better provision for social security. This would be another cause for a decline in the number of births in a society. In other words, the utility of the welfare factor (C') is also expressed by a downward slope. Adding these three factors together, the total utility of having children decreases as the economy develops.

In contrast, the disutility of having and raising children increases as a result of economic development. First, with respect to the direct cost, as the economy develops the living standards also improve and parents would be required to provide better shelter and food for their children. Should the period for parents to send their children to school become longer through compulsory education and other social conditions, parents would incur an even larger direct cost. Even if the government subsidizes much of the educational costs through increased budgetary allocation to the education sector, the prolonged educational period still implies longer dependency of children on parents, which results in greater cost of raising children. Indicating this disutility or cost of raising children along the vertical axis of Figure 2.2, the direct cost (A) is represented by a rising slope.

Second, with respect to the indirect cost, it is reasonable to assume an upward slope indicating increasing indirect or opportunity cost of raising children (B in Figure 2.2). The reason for this is that as the economy develops, there are more employment opportunities for mothers to earn greater cash income, and this income is forfeited by mothers in order to give birth to and raise children; in other words, the indirect or opportunity cost of having children increases in proportion to the growth in per capita income.

By aggregating these three factors of utility and the two factors of disutility in Figure 2.2, we obtain Figure 2.3. In this figure, if per capita income level exceeds y*, the disutility of having an additional child (A+B) becomes greater than its utility (A'+B'+C'), and assuming one makes a rational decision, the couple would not have an additional child. Professor Harvey Leibenstein explained this mechanism using Figure 2.4. U_n and U_{n-1} indicate the utility of having the nth and the (n–1)th child, respectively, and D_n and D_{n-1} represent their disutility. It is assumed that the utility of having the nth child is less than that of the (n–1)th child, and the disutility of having the nth child is greater than that of the (n–1)th child.

When a society's income level is low and it is below y^1, the utility of having the nth child, U_n, exceeds the disutility, D_n, and parents would rationally decide to have an additional nth child. When its income level is above y^1, the disutility, D_n, becomes larger than the utility, U_n, and parents should decide to not have the nth child. An increase in income level thus decreases the number of births per family in this society by one. If the income level increases further and exceeds y^2, even for the (n–1)th child its disutility, D_{n-1}, would be larger than the utility, U_{n-1}. Under this condition, parents would opt not to have the (n–1)th child and society as a whole would have two less children per family than what it could expect at an income level below y^1. Through this process, the expected number of children per family decreases from n to (n–1), and then to (n–2) as income level increases.

Figure 2.3 UTILITY AND DISUTILITY OF HAVING AN ADDITIONAL CHILD (II)

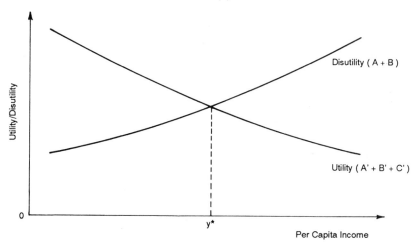

Figure 2.4 UTILITY AND DISUTILITY OF HAVING AN ADDITIONAL CHILD (III)

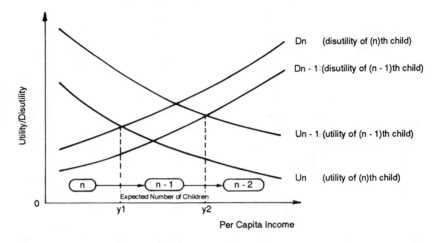

SOURCE :   H. Leibenstein. 1974. An Interpretation of Economic Theory of Fertility: Promising
Path or Blind Alley? *Journal of Economic Literature* 12 (2).

What Causes Birth Rates to Decline?

It is not easy to prove the validity of the theory of population economics that
we have been discussing. However, this proposition appears to have great
relevance in analyzing population movements in Asian countries. In this
connection, we may consider the following four issues.

First, with respect to the income factor of the utility of having an additional child, the economic value of children or their contribution to household income is indeed significant, especially in poor agrarian societies in
Asia. This may be one reason why birth rates are high in South Asia and in
certain Southeast Asian countries while they are low in the Asian NIEs. In a
rural society, children are expected to perform various household chores such
as collecting firewood, fetching water, taking care of domestic animals, and
looking after their younger brothers and sisters. They also work hard to assist
in productive labor in many different ways, and their participation in the
work of the family during the farming season, especially in sowing and cultivation, is extremely important. A study reports that on average, a child of 6
to 8 years of age in rural Nepal works 3 to 4 hours per day. In Bangladesh,
boys of landless farmers in the Mymensingh region in the age group of 10 to
12 are reported to work an average of 5 hours per day while girls between 13
to 15 years of age work 3.5 hours per day. A World Bank report states that the
income levels of teenagers in the slums in the Philippines are often compara-

ble to those of the adults. In contrast, we seldom see working children in countries such as South Korea, Taiwan, Hong Kong, and Singapore, where the society is rapidly changing through industrialization. In these countries, there were many working children until only about 10 years ago.

The second point concerns the disutility or the cost of having an additional child. As a country advances through industrialization, workers are required to have additional knowledge on various matters. This is true not only for those engaged in the industrial or service sectors but also for those working as farmers. As a farmer in a modern industrialized society, one must have knowledge of fertilizers, agricultural chemicals including pesticides, seeds, agricultural machinery, and irrigation and drainage; the farmer must also be familiar with other matters such as agricultural cooperative associations and agricultural finance. Having a basic level of scientific and vocational knowledge becomes extremely important and it is absolutely essential to have literacy and numeracy. In other words, industrialization requires children to be better equipped through education, and the consequential increase in educational costs makes a decline in the number of births in a given society inevitable. As can be seen from Figure 2.5, there is a significant relationship between birth rates and secondary school enrollment rates which have a predominant influence on the formation of skilled workers in a country. Among the Asian countries, there is also a clear relationship between the secondary school enrollment rate and the generally anticipated degree of industrialization. Each of the four groups, i.e., Japan, the NIEs, the Southeast Asian countries, and the South Asian countries, occupies a distinct position in Figure 2.5.

Third, the higher educational level required as a result of industrialization would affect the structure of the labor market. As a society becomes industrialized, the relative size of the labor force that work as small farmers, unskilled workers, retailers, and workers of manual industries becomes smaller as compared to that of those working as office managers, professionals, white-collar workers, and skilled workers. Entry into the former group of jobs is relatively easy for a young worker while entry into the latter group is extremely difficult. This change in labor market structure also results in a marked contrast where countries with high birth rates tend to have a low ratio of skilled workers, while in developed countries the birth rates are notably lower and the shares of skilled workers in the entire labor are relatively high (Figure 2.6).

The indirect cost of having a child is the fourth point. Economic development stimulates the demand for labor and increases in the wage level, both of which tend to encourage women's participation in the labor market. This, in turn, increases the opportunity cost of a woman staying home and raising children, and has the effect of reducing the number of children. While the

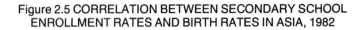

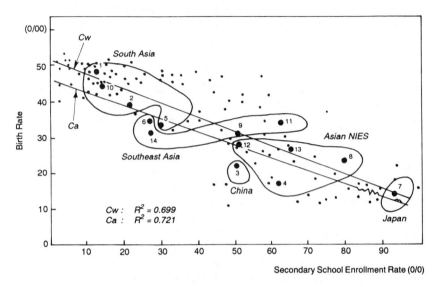

Figure 2.5 CORRELATION BETWEEN SECONDARY SCHOOL
ENROLLMENT RATES AND BIRTH RATES IN ASIA, 1982

NOTES :   Cw: Regression based on the worldwide statistics
             Ca: Regression based on the statistics of Asian countries

COUNTRIES: 1   Bangladesh
              2   Myanmar (Burma)
              3   China
              4   Hong Kong
              5   India
              6   Indonesia
              7   Japan
              8   South Korea
              9   Malaysia
             10   Pakistan
             11   Philippines
             12   Singapore
             13   Sri Lanka
             14   Thailand

SOURCES :   United Nations. *Demographic Yearbook*. New York: UN; United Nations Educational,
             Scientific, and Cultural Organization. *Statistical Yearbook*. Geneva: UNESCO.

data are not sufficient to clearly show a distinct relationship between birth
rates and the participation rates of women in the labor force, Figure 2.7 sug-
gests that there is a clear relationship between the two. Moreover as shown in
Figure 2.8, there is a significant relationship between birth rates and female
secondary school enrollment rates; an increase in women's participation rate
in the labor force is positively correlated with an increase in educational levels of women.

Through these mechanisms, industrialization of a country, as measured by

Figure 2.6 CORRELATION BETWEEN THE RATIO OF SKILLED WORKERS IN THE TOTAL LABOR FORCE AND BIRTH RATES IN ASIA, 1982

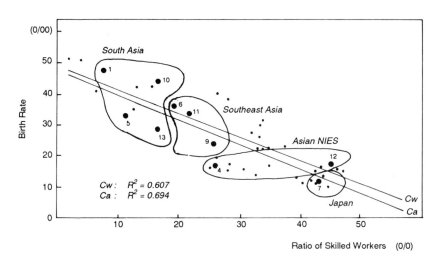

NOTES :   Ratio of skilled workers implies the share of professionals, engineers, administrators, white-collar workers and those engaged in sales out of the total labor force.

Cw: Regression based on worldwide statistics
Ca: Regression based on Asian countries

COUNTRIES: 1   Bangladesh
              2   Myanmar (Burma)
              3   China
              4   Hong Kong
              5   India
              6   Indonesia
              7   Japan
              8   South Korea
              9   Malaysia
              10   Pakistan
              11   Philippines
              12   Singapore
              13   Sri Lanka
              14   Thailand

SOURCES :   United Nations. *Demographic Yearbook*. New York: UN; International Labour Organization. *Yearbook of Labour Statistics*. Geneva: ILO.

various indicators such as an increase in income level, a higher technological level, a larger proportion of skilled workers, an increase in the participation rate of women in the labor force, and higher educational levels of women, diminishes the economic value of children while concurrently increases the direct educational cost and the indirect opportunity cost of raising children. It is these social forces which influence parents' choice to have fewer children, which results in a reduction of the birth rate of the society. There is a

Figure 2.7 CORRELATION BETWEEN THE PARTICIPATION RATE OF WOMEN IN THE LABOR FORCE AND BIRTH RATES IN ASIA, 1982

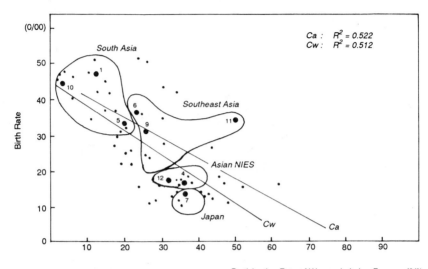

Participation Rate of Women in Labor Force   (0/0)

NOTES :   Cw: Regression based on worldwide statistics
           Ca: Regression based on Asian countries

COUNTRIES: 1 Bangladesh
             2 Myanmar (Burma)
             3 China
             4 Hong Kong
             5 India
             6 Indonesia
             7 Japan
             8 South Korea
             9 Malaysia
            10 Pakistan
            11 Philippines
            12 Singapore
            13 Sri Lanka
            14 Thailand

SOURCES : United Nations. *Demographic Yearbook*. New York: UN; United Nations
           Educational, Scientific, and Cultural Organization. *Statistical Yearbook*.
           Geneva: UNESCO.

sharp contrast between a society with these various social pressures and a pre-industrial society with a high birth rate which has hardly any social pressures of these kinds.

In the Asian NIEs, birth rates are steadily decreasing because of the various factors that were just discussed. Birth rates in the Southeast Asian countries have finally entered into a phase of decline. However in the South

Figure 2.8 CORRELATION BETWEEN FEMALE SECONDARY
SCHOOL ENROLLMENT RATES AND BIRTH RATES IN ASIA, 1982

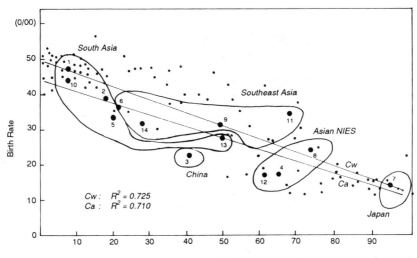

NOTES :   Cw: Regression based on worldwide statistics
            Ca: Regression based on Asian countries

COUNTRIES :   1   Bangladesh
               2   Myanmar (Burma)
               3   China
               4   Hong Kong
               5   India
               6   Indonesia
               7   Japan
               8   South Korea
               9   Malaysia
              10   Pakistan
              11   Philippines
              12   Singapore
              13   Sri Lanka
              14   Thailand

SOURCES :   United Nations. *Demographic Yearbook.* New York: UN; United Nations
             Educational, Scientific, and Cultural Organization. *Statistical Yearbook.*
             Geneva: UNESCO.

Asian countries today, only a very slight decline in birth rates has taken
place.

Figure 2.9 shows the demographic transition index as measured recently
by two demographers. A value of 1.0 in this index implies that a country has
completed the entire demographic transition process and has entered into
the final phase where both birth and death rates are low. If this value is close

Figure 2.9 DEMOGRAPHIC TRANSITION INDEX OF VARIOUS COUNTRIES, 1980

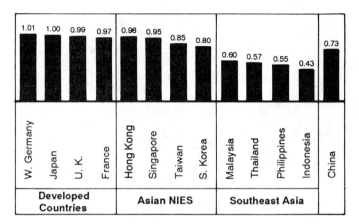

SOURCE :   Cho, L. T., and J. Y. Togashi. 1985. *Industrial Transition and Demographic Dynamics of the Asia-Pacific Region.* Paper presented at the International Symposium on the Role of the Asia-Pacific Region in World Economic Development, Nippon University, December 17–20, Tokyo.

to zero, it implies that a country has just entered into the process. Japan has already attained the value 1.0, and the Asian NIEs, led by Hong Kong, are rapidly approaching the level of Japan. In comparison, the demographic transition indexes of the Southeast Asian countries continue to lag behind that of the Asian NIEs and it may take some time for the former group to catch up with the levels of the latter. While figures for the South Asian countries are not included in these statistics, their indexes are likely to be much lower than those of the Southeast Asian countries.

The Effectiveness of Population Control Policies

In order to expedite the demographic transition, some Asian countries have pursued population control policies on a national scale. It is not hard to imagine that India, a typical country with excess population, has been actively promoting government-led family planning movements from early on. However, the initial actions that were taken under this policy failed to achieve any significant results, and in the mid-1970s, the government of India employed forced sterilization to control population growth, despite the fact that such a measure could possibly violate basic human rights. This attempt turned out to be a miserable failure, and some believe that Mrs.

Indira Gandhi's government was overthrown in March 1977 because of the enforcement of this sterilization policy.

It is an irony that India, which adopted and pursued population control policies from very early on, will probably be the last country in the region to experience a decline in its birth rate. On the other hand, South Korea, Taiwan, and Hong Kong were successful in drastically reducing birth rates without adopting any strict population control policies. What then went wrong in India? Comparing India with these three East Asian countries, it appears that a reduction in birth rates is unlikely to occur unless there are social pressures that induce a decline in birth rates which are generated by economic development itself. In other words, the theory illustrated in Figure 2.4 does exist and is applicable to Asian countries. The issues which population control policies should be dealing with are the ignorance of parents who do not know they can choose the number of children they wish to raise and who are not capable of making rational "economic" decisions by comparing the utility and disutility of children, the social and cultural obstacles preventing parents from making rational decisions, and the lack of means for parents to realize their rational decisions. Family planning policies should be used to support parents in making rational decisions, as well as support their decisions.

We may conclude that the relationship between the utility and disutility of having an additional child is influenced by economic development itself and population control policies can be utilized most effectively only when they are designed to supplement economic development. That economic development is the most effective factor in reducing population growth may be the most relevant proposition, and family planning or population control policies can never substitute for economic development.

China, however, can be considered to be an exception to this proposition; its uniqueness is illustrated in Figure 2.1. Even with low per capita income, China, which like India was characterized by excess population, did achieve a substantial reduction in the birth rate. This decline in fertility was primarily the result of a strict population control policy that had been followed since 1978. The slogan used to promote the policy was "late marriage, late childbearing, fewer births." "Late marriage" implies delaying marriage for more than three years after reaching the legal marriageable age of 22 years for men and 20 years for women. "Late childbearing" means giving birth only after reaching 24 years of age. "Fewer births" implies the principle of "one child for one couple" which is to be observed by civil servants and residents in urban areas.

This population control policy has been very strictly implemented in China. After having the first child, if a couple declares that they will not have a second child or if one of the couple is sterilized, they are given a certificate for having only one child and are entitled to receive various preferential treatments such as medical benefits. On the other hand, if a couple has a second child, they are penalized through a reduction in salary or by other means and for the third child they are even more severely punished. As a result, it is reported that in Beijing, for example, almost 100 percent of the children entering into the primary schools in recent years have been the first child of their parents.

In a country like China, where there is an extensive administrative network of the national Communist Party authorities, this kind of population control policy was certainly effective. The population pyramids of 1953, 1964, and 1982 are shown in Figure 2.10. The first two pyramids represent the age distribution of the population before the enforcement of the policy and the last pyramid represents the age distribution after the introduction of the policy. The effect of the rigidly enforced population control policy is clear from these pyramids.

However, it is still not yet certain whether China's population control policies will be successful in the long run. There is still resistance to the "fewer births" policy especially in rural China, as many people are maintaining the traditional beliefs such as "many children means greater happiness," "a family perishes without a child," or "early childbearing brings a superior child." Second, if the "fewer births" or one-child policy is to be maintained for a prolonged period of time, it would inevitably result in a serious change in population structure. There would eventually be an extremely large proportion of elders. In an extreme case, we may consider a family composition of 4-2-1, i.e., a family consisting of four grandparents, two parents, and one child. At the same time that there are fewer children becoming economically active adults, the majority of the population will be getting older and the population structure of Chinese society will change with an increased proportion of old people. This situation is in contrast to the problem of a rising dependency burden due to the increasing number of youthful dependents in developing countries (which was discussed in Chapter 1). Instead, what we are witnessing is an increase in the elderly dependency ratio in China. We have yet to see how well China will be able to deal with this increasing burden of elderly dependents in the future.

The third issue is the revival of the household farming system in China following the collapse of the collective farming system organized under the People's Communes (this issue will be discussed further in Chapter 10). Under the People's Communes system, farmers received egalitarian distribution of the revenue of their commune. This meant that each farmer received more or less the same salary regardless of the amount of time and effort the farmer devoted. As a result, there were few incentives for farmers to increase

Figure 2.10 POPULATION PYRAMIDS OF CHINA

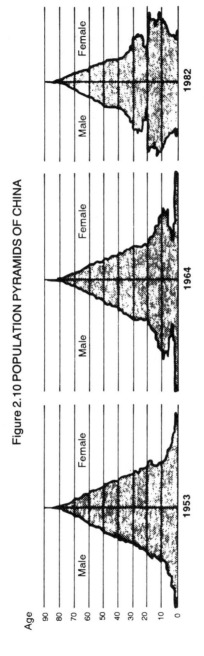

Age

90
80
70
60
50
40
30
20
10
0

1953   Male   Female

1964   Male   Female

1982   Male   Female

SOURCE :   China, National Bureau of Statistics. *Statistical Yearbook of China*. Beijing: NBS.

production. However, under today's household farming system, the harder the farmers work, the more they can earn. This also implies that there is a strong incentive for farmers to have more children as a means to have additional working members in their families in order to produce more for greater income. Accordingly, there is now a social pressure towards an increase in the farming population. In view of all of these factors, it may still be premature to conclude, even from the experiment in China, whether population control policies are truly effective or not.

CHAPTER THREE

Polarization of the Peasantry

Absolute Poverty

Along with a rapid population increase, most of the Asian countries have experienced a contraction in the boundaries for land cultivation. The growth in population has inevitably brought about fragmentation of arable land which works to further reduce the already low level of farmers' income. Furthermore, farmers who cannot sustain their standards of living by cultivating the fragmented land have been forced to sell their plots of land. Consequently, there has been a downward polarization of peasantry through degradation from landed farmers to tenants and finally to "landless workers" who do not even hold the rights to cultivate the land.

Of course, there is always another side of the coin. If arable land becomes scarce under population pressure, a country will be tempted to increase fertilizer inputs or to create and disseminate a high-fertilizer, high-yielding improved variety which will increase hectare yield and thereby utilize the scarce arable land more efficiently. Indeed, such a campaign did take place and the Green Revolution, which saw the introduction of a high-yielding variety of rice to Asia, positively influenced Asian agriculture.

In viewing the current status of Asian agriculture, it is important for us to understand the two sides of the coin or the interaction of two opposite forces; namely, the decline in farmers' incomes owing to population pressure and the rise in farmers' incomes due to technological progress in agriculture. This chapter discusses these two forces further.

In South Asian countries such as Bangladesh and India, which are historically known as overpopulated countries, the area of arable land has not increased at all in the past decade (Table 3.1). And although there has been some expansion of arable land in Southeast Asian countries such as Indonesia and the Philippines, it has been matched by an increase in agricultural population, and as a result, these countries continue to face severe land constraints.

A consequence of population increase and the scarcity of cultivable land is the fragmentation of arable land which has also been intensified by the traditional system of equal inheritance. The South Asian countries show a dramatic pattern toward land fragmentation. In Bangladesh, for example, a comparison of four agricultural census periods shows that the area of arable

31

Table 3.1
Agriculture-Related Indices of Selected Asian Countries
(1974 – 1976 = 100)

COUNTRY	INDEX OF ARABLE LAND AREA (A)		INDEX OF AGRICULTURAL POPULATION (B)		(A/B)	
	1980	1984	19890	1984	1980	1984
Bangladesh	100	100	110	120	91	83
India	100	100	109	119	92	84
Indonesia	100	106	103	104	97	102
Philippines	111	115	111	120	100	96

SOURCE: Food and Agriculture Organization. *Production Yearbook.* Rome: FAO.

land per farm household declined by 35 percent between 1960 and 1977. Such fragmentation of arable land is reflected in the increased portion of very small farm households to total farm households. In Figure 3.1, which shows the percentage share of farm households owning a certain number of acres, it can be seen that the percentage share of farmers owning less than two acres of land increased sharply from 37 percent in 1960 to 65 percent in 1977.

Under this process of land subdivision, maintenance of farmers' standards of living has become increasingly difficult. A comprehensive rural survey in Bangladesh of more than 10,000 farm households was conducted from late 1973 to early 1974. This survey showed relatively low food self-sufficiency rates of farm households, i.e., to what extent farm households could meet their demand for food in a year through cultivating their own land (Figure 3.2). Sixty-three percent of the farm households surveyed could produce only less than three months' demand of their own food consumption. Moreover, the ratio of farm households under absolute poverty, i.e., households with less than 1,805 calorie intake per person per day, is considerably high, and has been gradually increasing since the mid-1960s (Figure 3.3).

Such impoverishment has forced farmers to sell their land and become farm workers whose final resort is to sell their own labor. These farm workers, who are engaged in various farm work such as tilling, leveling, planting, weeding, harvesting, and threshing, receive wages as day laborers during the busy season. During the off-farm season, they earn a living by working as peddlers, brokers, carpenters, wheeldrivers, and housemaids. They are the poorest group in a rural society. According to the *1977 Land Occupancy Survey of Rural Bangladesh* of the Bangladesh government, the number of workers' households accounted for 33 percent of total farm households.

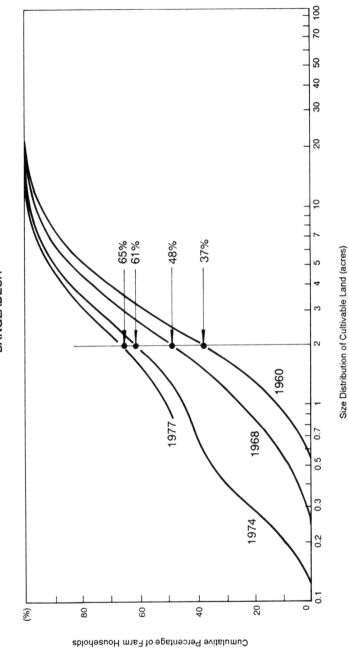

Figure 3.1 CUMULATIVE PERCENTAGE OF FARM HOUSEHOLDS BY SIZE OF CULTIVABLE LAND, BANGLADESH

Size Distribution of Cultivable Land (acres)

Cumulative Percentage of Farm Households

SOURCE : Bangladesh Bureau of Statistics. *Summary Report of the 1977 Land Occupancy Survey of Rural Bangladesh*. Dacca: BOS.

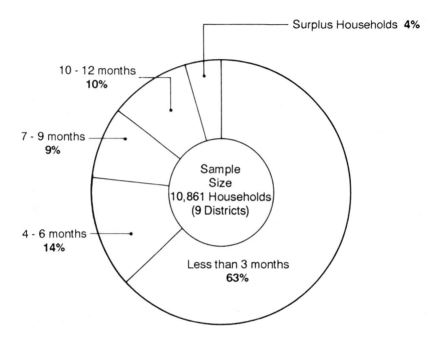

Figure 3.2 FOOD SUFFICIENCY RATES OF FARM HOUSEHOLDS IN
BANGLADESH, 1973–1974

SOURCE :   Bangladesh Institute of Development Studies. 1977. *Famine 1974: Political Economy
of Mass Starvation in Bangladesh*. Dacca: BIDS.

Emergence of the Farm Workers

A similar phenomenon has emerged in Southeast Asian countries such as the
Philippines and Indonesia. The Philippines is a country with haciendas
(large-scale land holdings). In Central Luzon, which is the rice basket of the
Philippines and is located in the hinterland of Metro Manila, tenant farmers
(including leaseholders) account for as much as 80 percent of the population. It is not difficult to believe that population pressure under such conditions has generated a massive supply of farm workers. Although official statistics on the Philippines' farm workers are not available, a case study
conducted by Masao Kikuchi in a village in Laguna (a province in the Southern Tagalog region) found that the ratio of farm workers' households to total
farm households increased from 31 percent in 1966, to 51 percent in 1976,
and to 63 percent in 1980.

At the same time, Kikuchi made an interesting observation about how
the number of farm workers have increased. The increase in farm households

Figure 3.3 PROPORTIONS OF FARM HOUSEHOLDS IN
ABSOLUTE POVERTY, BANGLADESH

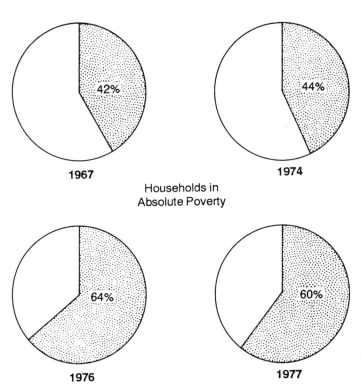

1967

1974

Households in
Absolute Poverty

1976

1977

SOURCE :   World Bank. 1980. *Bangladesh. Current Economic Position and Short Term Outlook.*
New York: WB.

in a certain village was brought about either by the creation of new independent households through parent-child inheritance or by settlement of
migrants from other villages. In a village where expansion of arable land is
not possible, some of the children are compelled to become farm workers
owing to the fact that the land to be inherited is limited (regardless of
whether it is owner-cultivated land or tenanted land). And in the case of
migrants who move into a village where no cultivable frontier exists, there is
very little choice but to be farm workers seeking employment opportunities.
At closer inspection of the data, of a total of 109 households in 1976, 75
became independent of their parents and the remaining 34 households were
migrants (Table 3.2). Of the former households, the proportion of farm
worker households increased yearly; 13 out of 19 households who became
independent of their parents in 1970–1976 were farm workers. The share of

Table 3.2

Emergence of Farm Workers in a Laguna Village, Philippines
(number of households)

| YEAR | INDEPENDENT FARM | | | IN-MIGRATION FARM | | | |
	FARMERS (1)	WORKERS (2)	TOTAL (3)	FARMERS (4)	WORKERS (5)	TOTAL (6)	TOTAL (3+6)
Prior to 1939	11	0	11	1	1	2	13
1940–1949	6	2	8	1	4	5	13
1950–1959	8	7	15	2	1	3	18
1960–1969	14	8	22	5	2	7	29
1970–1976	6	13	19	3	14	17	36
Total	45	30	75	12	22	34	109

SOURCE: Kikuchi, Masao. 1978. *Firipin Noson ni Okeru Seido-teki Henka-Raguna-shu Ichi Komesaku Noson no Jirei Bunseki* [Institutional changes in a Philippine village: A case study of a rice village in Laguna]. *Nogyo Sogo Kenkyu* [Quarterly journal of agriculture] 32(3).

farm worker households in total migrant households became higher as time passed.

A massive supply of farm workers in rural areas naturally brings about a downward pressure on wages. (Here again we have to base our arguments on individual village survey data owing to lack of statistics on farm wages in the countries.) According to a survey in the Philippines, the real daily wage of a farm worker, deflated by the price of rice per kilogram, declined from 14.0 pesos in 1960 to 10.1 pesos in 1977.

The accumulation of farm workers, who are the poorest in the rural areas, together with the decline in wages has inevitably brought about unequal distribution of income. The changes in the income distribution of Filipino farmers are shown in Lorenz curves which indicate the percentage of total income that is earned by a certain percentage of the poorest group (Figure 3.4). The Lorenz curves show that the percentage of farm income earned by the lowest 40 percent of the farmers declined noticeably over the years. Despite the average annual growth rate of 1.8 percent in farm household income from 1957 to 1975, there was a large and growing inequality in the distribution of income and the emergence of a massive number of farmers under absolute poverty cannot be ignored. According to a survey conducted by the Development Academy of the Philippines, the proportion of farmers who could not meet the subsistence level of living (which includes food and other basic needs) increased from 75 percent in 1965 to 85 percent in 1975.

Land subdivision in Java villages, where both the population growth rate and the ratio of small holdings are very high even in the Asian context, is a serious matter. Although there are no official statistics, farm workers are

Figure 3.4 LORENZ CURVES OF PHILIPPINE FARM HOUSEHOLDS

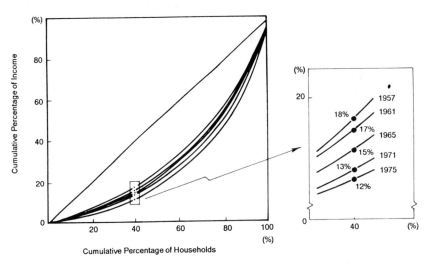

SOURCE :   Government of the Philippines. *Family Income and Expenditure*. Manila.

believed to be accumulating on a large scale. Table 3.3, which summarizes twenty samples of rural surveys conducted in various regions of Java, shows that the percentage of farm worker households in each surveyed village varied from a low of 10 percent to a high of 89 percent with an average as high as 54 percent. A significant correlation between population density of the villages and the ratio of farm worker population has also been observed. Population pressure on scarce arable land has inevitably created a massive number of farm workers through the downward polarization of peasantry.

Consequences of the Green Revolution

The so-called polarization of farmers is one social force which rules Asian rural societies in which frontier land has been lost and in which rates of population growth continue to be high. Nevertheless, as mentioned earlier, there are two sides to a coin. It should also be noted that another countervailing force has also begun to develop. Both scarcity of land and accumulation of surplus labor encouraged the development of land-saving and labor-intensive agricultural technologies. This is epitomized by the development and introduction of high-yielding varieties of rice in the Green Revolution.

Indica is a rice variety that was traditionally cultivated in Asia primarily because it was well-suited to the conditions of Asian paddy cultivation. Rice farming in Asia has historically depended on flood and rainfed water and

Table 3.3
Landless Laborers in Java, Indonesia

VILLAGES SURVEYED	SURVEY YEAR	POPULATION DENSITY (KM²)	RATIO OF LANDLESS LABORERS TO POPULATION (%)
A Village (East Java)	1977	331	45
B Village (East Java)	1977	605	63
C Village (East Java)	1976	1,143	49
D Village (East Java)	1972	1,252	82
E Village (Central Java)	1977	615	11
F Village (Central Java)	1977	1,014	25
G Village (Central Java)	1977	4,264	89
H Village (Central Java)	1977	1,317	43
I Village (Central Java)	1977	978	33
J Village (Central Java)	1977	1,738	70
K Village (Central Java)	1977	1,223	67
L Village (Central Java)	1970	na	37
M Village (West Java)	1958	556	67
N Village (West Java)	1958	347	10
O Village (West Java)	1976	1,331	65
P Village (East Java)	1978	754	60
Q Village (East Java)	1977	980	45
R Village (Central Java)	1978	1,154	83
S Village (Central Java)	1976	543	63
T Village (Central Java)	1976	1,043	67
Average		1,115	54

SOURCE: Collier, W. L. 1979. Declining Labor Absorption (1878–1980) in Javanese Rice Production. *Kajian Ekonomi Malaysia* [Journal of the Malaysian economic association] 16(1/2).

much less on irrigation. It was thus essential to plant rice in deep-water fields for continuing rice cultivation to avoid water shortage during the dry season in areas with poor irrigation facilities. It was also necessary to plant a variety with a high stalk and thick foliage in order to overcome the growing weeds. The indica variety with its generic characteristics of a long stalk and thick foliage was ideal for Asia's paddies.

However, the palay yield (palay/straw ratio) of the indica variety is low because the variety lodged too easily before harvesting. Per hectare rice yield in Asia was about one-third that of Japan in the early 1960s. Application of fertilizer to the traditional varieties to increase yield only resulted in excessive foliage and lodging during the season of ears. Thus, the increased application of fertilizers to the traditional varieties did not result in high yields.

With Asian agriculture in such a condition, the Rockefeller and Ford Foundations undertook strenuous research efforts on the development of high-yield varieties (HYVs) by establishing the International Rice Research

Institute (IRRI) in 1960 on the premises of the College of Agriculture at the University of the Philippines in Los Baños (about 25 miles [40 km] to the south of Manila). IRRI succeeded in developing a new series of HYVs of rice (the IR series) which were characterized by short and strong stalks with improved lodging resistance. Furthermore, the HYVs' upright foliage made efficient photosynthesis possible. The HYVs brought a substantially higher per hectare yield compared to the traditional varieties. Subsequent HYVs were successively improved and introduced to the Asian paddy fields.

The percentage of the area planted with HYVs in the latest year reached 85 percent in the Philippines and 64 percent in Indonesia (Table 3.4). As a result, rice yield per hectare in each Asian country began to increase very rapidly (Table 3.5). It was the first time in Asian history of rice cultivation that a marked increase in yield per hectare was realized in such a short period of time.

Another important fact is that HYVs are more labor absorptive than are the traditional rice varieties. If HYVs generate a strong labor-absorptive power, it should be highly welcomed in rural Asia where surplus labor exists and an increasing number of farm workers are being created through downward polarization of peasantry. Table 3.6 is an excerpt from a summary

Table 3.4
Area of High-Yielding Rice Varieties as a Share of Total Paddy Area in Selected Asian Countries (percentage)

COUNTRY	1967	1970	1973	1976	1979	1983
Bangladesh	1	5	16	14	20	25[a]
India	5	15	26	35	41	53
Indonesia	–	10	27	35	45	64
Philippines	21	50	63	67	76	85

NOTE: a. 1982.
SOURCE: International Rice Research Institute. *World Rice Statistics*. Manila: IRRI.

Table 3.5
Land Productivity of Rice in Selected Asian Countries (kg/ha, 1968 = 100)

COUNTRY	1968	1970	1975	1980	1985
Bangladesh	100	97	106	116	125
India	100	104	115	124	142
Indonesia	100	111	123	154	186
Philippines	100	129	129	167	199

SOURCE: Food and Agriculture Organization. *Production Yearbook*. Rome: FAO.

Table 3.6
Labor Absorption Rates of HYVs in Rice-Growing
Areas in Asia (man days/ha)

COUNTRY	LABOR ABSORPTION RATES
Bangladesh (Mymensingh)	1.42
India (Ferozepur)	1.16
Indonesia (Java)	1.11
Pakistan (Hyderabad)	1.18
Philippines (Laguna)	1.28
South Korea (Hwasunggun)	1.10
Thailand (Don Chedi, Suphan Buri)	1.44

SOURCE: Barker, B., and V. Cordova. 1978. Labor Utilization in Rice Production. In *Economic Consequences of the New Rice Technology*. Los Banos: IRRI.

report of country surveys on labor inputs used in producing rice of HYVs and traditional varieties. Despite some degree of variation, it appears that HYVs are more labor absorptive than the traditional varieties in all countries.

The reason why the HYVs were more labor absorptive than the traditional varieties is related to a marked increase in demand for labor that are employed in simple work such as weeding and land preparation which intensified with the introduction of HYVs. Table 3.7 compares labor inputs utilized in 1965 before the introduction of HYVs and two periods after the introduction of HYVs in Laguna. The increase in the amount of labor employed in simple farm work, who were the poorest group of workers in the village, is particularly large. The increase of fertilizer inputs associated with the introduction of HYVs encouraged the growth of weeds which made weeding work more important. Furthermore, the necessity to apply fertilizer regularly encouraged intensive weeding work which caused the sharp increase in dependency on employed labor force.

The introduction of HYVs contributed to the progress of Asian agriculture not only through increased productivity of scarce land, but also through absorption of surplus labor. Nevertheless, there continue to be problems related to pervasive increases in population and the associated polarization of peasantry. Thus the supply of labor has been continuing to exceed the demand for labor which was augmented by the Green Revolution. Good evidence of this argument is that the real wage of Asian farm workers has not yet shown signs of an increasing trend. For example, consider Figure 3.5 which shows the index of real wages of farm workers in selected Asian countries. Although we cannot draw a definite conclusion owing to the statistical

Table 3.7
Labor Use in Rice Production in Laguna, Philippines[a] (work days/ha)

FARMING OPERATIONS	FAMILY LABOR				HIRED LABOR				TOTAL LABOR[b]			
	1965	1970	1975	1978	1965	1970	1975	1978	1965	1970	1975	1978
Land preparation	14.4	5.7	4.5	2.7	4.0	5.1	6.0	6.5	19.2	11.4	10.6	9.2
Repair and cleaning of dikes	3.8	3.8	3.5	3.3	0.2	0.9	1.1	1.5	4.2	4.9	4.7	5.2
Transplanting	0.2	0.0	0.0	0.0	9.6	10.6	11.3	10.0	9.8	10.7	11.3	10.0
Weeding	9.0	6.7	5.9	4.8	2.1	12.1	25.6	21.8	11.1	19.1	31.6	26.6
Fertilizing and spraying	0.9	1.5	2.3	1.7	0.0	0.1	0.5	0.7	0.9	1.6	3.0	2.6
Other preharvest operations[c]	3.7	7.5	4.9	3.6	0.7	1.5	9.7	0.4	4.5	9.1	14.7	4.2
Total preharvest labor	32.0	25.2	21.1	16.1	16.6	30.3	54.2	40.9	49.7	56.8	75.9	57.8
Harvesting, threshing, and postharvest activities	0.5	1.6	0.8	0.7	34.6	35.7	35.0	27.1	35.8	37.3	35.8	27.8
Total labor	32.5	26.8	21.9	16.8	51.2	66.0	89.2	68.0	85.5	94.1	111.7	85.6

NOTES: a. During wet season.

  b. Includes exchange labor.

  c. Seed bed preparation, pulling and rolling seedlings, and replanting.

SOURCE: Smith, J., and F. Gascon. 1979. *The Effect of the New Rice Technology on Family Labor Utilization in Laguna.* IRRI Research Paper Series, No. 42. Manila: IRRI.

Figure 3.5 INDEX OF REAL WAGES OF AGRICULTURAL LABORERS IN SELECTED ASIAN COUNTRIES

(1965 = 100 before 1974, 1975 = 100 after 1974)

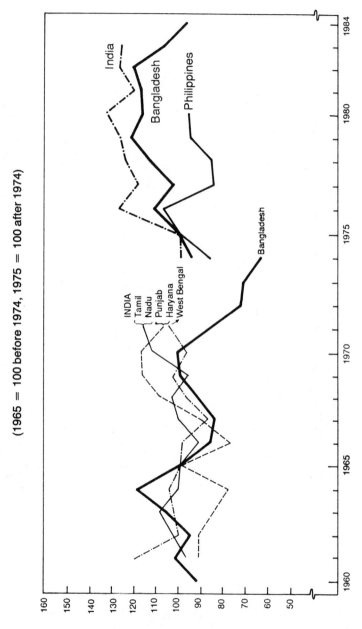

SOURCES : Asian Development Bank. 1978. *Rural Asia - Challenge and Opportunity*. New York: Praeger; United Nations, Economic and Social Commission for Asia and the Pacific. *Statistical Yearbook for Asia and the Pacific*. Bangkok: ESCAP.

deficiencies, we can infer from the figure that farm workers in the countries observed continue to live under harsh conditions.

In order to make agricultural development in Asia a success, surplus labor must be significantly reduced. Asian NIEs such as Korea and Taiwan are typical countries which have achieved great success in agricultural development. The success was brought about by a speedy absorption of agricultural surplus labor into the nonagricultural sector, particularly into the industrial sector. This does, of course, apply equally to the case of Japan. The experiences of agricultural development in both the Asian NIEs and Japan are discussed in Chapter 5.

CHAPTER FOUR

Changes and Conflicts in the
Traditional Society

Agricultural Involution and Shared Poverty

In the previous chapter, we examined the subdivision of arable land associated with population increase which resulted in the downward polarization of peasantry. This trend is not only important in the context of the degradation of farmers' economic status, but is also important to the extent that this will change the customs and systems of Asian traditional communal societies which thereby increases the danger of instability in rural societies to which we should pay much attention.

The Asian farmers have, for many centuries, lived and worked in a community of neighbors and kin based upon the principle of mutual help. Sociopolitical stability of the Asian society has been based upon the stability of rural communal societies. The very foundation of this stability, however, has been eroding rapidly. In this chapter, we will review how customs and systems have contributed to the stability of rural communal societies and what factors are responsible for endangering this stability.

In his thesis on Javanese society, anthropologist Professor Clifford Geertz proposed a model of possible traditional rural communal societies in Asia based upon the concepts of "agricultural involution" and "shared poverty" through the observations of high labor absorption of paddy rice compared to other crops and the mechanism of income distribution through mutual help in the rural communal societies. Agricultural involution is a pattern of agricultural production which seeks to maximize yield per hectare by applying maximum labor to a given plot of arable land without changing the methods of rice cultivation. Although the per capita economic pie is divided to its limit as a result, polarization of peasantry never occurred. Rather, according to Geertz's model of Javanese society, farmers have managed to maintain stable and harmonious communal societies through equal distribution of a limited, divided pie or through shared poverty. This thesis made a strong impact not only on the study of Javanese villages, but on all research efforts that examined rural societies of Southeast Asia.

Geertz first observed the ecologically strong labor absorptive capacity of paddy rice production. The production process includes land cultivation, leveling, irrigation, drainage, seed management, broadcasting, planting, weeding, harvesting, threshing, and other extensive tasks. Furthermore, these tasks are repeatedly performed during the year through double- and triple-cropping cultivation in some areas. In addition, other tasks associated with wet-rice cultivation, such as construction and management of dams, ponds, waterways, dikes, and wells, are required. In wet-rice cultivation, which involves a variety of diverse tasks, a small absorption of labor in each work process amounts to the creation of considerable employment opportunities as a whole. Geertz's finding was that the Javanese farmers could absorb the increase in population under such ecological conditions of wet-rice cultivation.

> Wet-rice cultivation, with its extraordinary ability to maintain levels of marginal labor productivity by always managing to work one more man in without a serious fall in per capita income, soaked up almost the whole of the additional population that Western intrusion created, at least indirectly. It is this ultimately self-defeating process that I have proposed to call "agricultural involution" (Geertz, C. 1963. *Agricultural Involution: The Process of Ecological Change in Indonesia.* Berkeley and Los Angeles: University of California Press, p. 80)

If agricultural involution is regarded as a solution to the Javanese farmers on the production side, shared poverty is considered to be a solution on the distribution side. Geertz's study of Javanese villages do not show the same kind of downward polarization of peasantry brought about by the fragmentation of arable land associated with population pressure that was discussed in the last chapter. Rather in a Javanese society, communal customs and systems, which allow the equal distribution of land for cultivation and equal employment opportunity among farmers, have been persistently maintained. Because of these systems, farmers could mutually share the reduced employment opportunities brought about by population pressure. In this context, Geertz found that there was a personal relationship which enabled the farmers to share poverty.

> With the steady growth of population came also the elaboration and extension of mechanisms through which agricultural product was spread, if not altogether evenly, at least relatively so, throughout the huge human horde which was obliged to subsist on it. Under the pressure of increasing numbers and limited resources Javanese village society did not bifurcate, as did that of so many other "underdeveloped" nations, into a group of large landlords and a group of oppressed near-serfs. Rather it maintained a comparatively high degree of social and economic homogeneity by dividing the economic pie into a steadily increasing number of minute pieces, a process to which I have referred elsewhere as "shared poverty" (Geertz 1963, p. 97)

It has been said that the richer farmers are obligated to provide employment opportunities to the poorer farmers, while the latter claim the right to obtain employment opportunities. For instance, Geertz observed that a landowner would lease a parcel of his land to a tenant farmer, while the landowner himself would work as a tenant in the lands of other farmers. Furthermore, Geertz observed an intricate relationship whereby a tenant rerented his tenanted land to another farmer. A multitudinous web of "exchange relationship of labor" was also practiced in such a way that harvesting workers contracted for rice planting and weeding tasks would subcontract the tasks to their kinsmen and neighbors. Through such communal customs and systems, the Javanese villages maintained a stable and harmonious society without peasant stratification despite the economic stagnation.

The Patron-Client Relationship

The next question is how could such a communal order be established? On this point, James Scott argues that the "moral norms" that guarantee subsistence requirements for all members have existed in the very foundation of the Southeast Asian village society. Because of these norms, a communal order or a "reciprocal" social order—reciprocal in the sense that among the farmers, help was always reciprocated—was established. Professor Scott explains how these moral norms came into existence.

Because most farmers in Southeast Asia live below a subsistence level of income, they are reluctant to accept a big change in their livelihood. Despite the low standard of living, their foremost concern is how to protect their subsistence level of living. In this sense, the behavioral principle of Southeast Asian farmers is "safety first" or "risk aversion"; thus the principle of profit maximization does not work. This behavioral principle of farmers is embodied in customs and personal human relations in villages. For instance, if a farmer for some reason fails to maintain his subsistence requirements, the farmer must seek help from other farmers. This will mean, however, that the farmer is obliged to extend his help when the other farmers face similar difficulties. This kind of reciprocity is nothing more than a risk avoidance scheme with the relationship of each farmer with the other farmers serving as the basis for sharing of risks. Professor Scott thinks that such "subsistence ethics" is shared by farmers and becomes the moral norms of the community.

Nevertheless, the members of the village community are not equal in their socioeconomic status. As a matter of fact, social stratification does exist, mainly according to the size of land ownership. Professor Scott, however, points out that such a class relationship among the poor village societies tends to be more like a relationship between the protector and the protected, or, in other words, a reciprocal relationship between patron and client rather than between the ruler and the ruled:

> The patron-client relationship—an exchange relationship between two roles— may be defined as a special case of dyadic (two-person) ties involving a largely instrumental friendship in which an individual of higher socio-economic status (patron) uses his own influence and resources to provide protection and/or benefits for a person of lower status (client) who, for his part, reciprocates by offering general support and assistance, including personal services, to the patron (Scott, James C. 1972. The Erosion of Patron-Client Bonds and Social Change in Rural Southeast Asia. *Journal of Asian Studies* 33(1), p. 8)

The patron provides employment opportunities, leases out cultivable land, and even takes care of seeds, agricultural tools, and marketing of farm products for his client. Furthermore, the patron arranges money for the client in times of economic distress such as sickness or accident, and he also solicits donations for weddings and funeral services, philanthropies, and school management. On the other hand, the client offers his labor services by participating in farm tasks at the request of the patron and also supports the political cause of the patron. In essence, the client seeks from the patron a guarantee for his subsistence requirements and the patron complies with the request. Through such a mechanism, the social status, the dignity, and the peace of both the patron and the client are secured in the communal society. According to Professor Scott, the moral norms of communal societies were sanctioned and accepted by both classes through this arrangement.

The relationship between the patron and client, however, is not always stable. Both patron and client might wish to attempt, if possible, to minimize obligations or conversely to maximize their individual rights. When these motives are revealed through actions, the foundation of reciprocal personal relations in communal societies collapses. In short, the most important factor which could shake the reciprocal relations is a weakening "bargaining position" of the farmers of lower status against the farmers of upper status. The bargaining position of tenant farmers or farm workers against the patron will naturally weaken as the pressure on land fragmentation and polarization of peasantry arising from the sharp increase in population becomes stronger and the number of tenant farmers or farm workers increases. If the number of tenant farmers who wish to lease land from landlords increases, then landlords can increase the rental or shorten the term of tenancy without much difficulty. The degradation and instability of the status of farm workers cannot be avoided. This will change the nature of communal societies that are based upon reciprocal relationships.

The change in patron-client relationships including diversified factors is shown in Table 4.1. The power relationship between the patron and client

Table 4.1

The Commercialization of Agriculture and the Balance of
Patron-Client Exchange

NATURE OF CHANGE	EFFECT ON PATRON-CLIENT RELATIONS
Growing inequality in landholding	Control of land becomes key basis of patronage; landholder's position strengthened in dealing with clients who seek access to narrowly held land
Population growth	Landholder's position strengthened in bargaining with a growing peasantry seeking access to land
Fluctuations in producer and consumer prices under commercial agriculture	Landholder's position strengthened as peasants increasingly need credit, relief, marketing assistance, etc.
Loss of "slack resources" (uncleared land, common pastorage, free fuel, etc.)	Loss of alternative security mechanisms weakens peasant-clients' bargaining position with patrons
Deterioration of village leveling mechanisms	Loss of alternative security mechanisms weakens peasant-clients' bargaining position with patrons
Colonial state protects property rights of land-owning classes	Landowner less in need of loyal local clientele; hence less incentive to maintain a balance of exchange that engenders legitimacy

SOURCE: Scott, J. C. 1972. The Erosion of Patron-Client Bonds and Social Change in Rural Southeast Asia. *Journal of Asian Studies* 30.

proceeds in such a way that the former gains at the expense of the latter, thereby necessitating changes in the reciprocal communal order of traditional village societies. Professor Scott saw that the protection and benefits given to the client by the patron were reduced while the patron's demand for the client's services becomes more oppressive and the patron-client relationship shifts to a more contractual and impersonal one.

Disappearance of *Ani-Ani* Knives

A typical case that is indicative of changes in village communal societies which are induced by population pressure is the change in Javanese rice harvesting systems which have attracted a great deal of interest from researchers on Indonesian studies in recent years. The traditional rice harvesting method in Java is to cut the stalks at about 20 centimeters below the panicles by using the *ani-ani*, a small knife which can be accommodated in the palm of one's hand.

There are several explanations why this inefficient method of harvesting has been widely practiced in Java. One explanation is the naive belief of gentle Javanese farmers that the use of the *ani-ani* prevents them from offending the goddess of rice. The *ani-ani* method has also been considered more appropriate than the rough cutting method of the sickle for harvesting the traditional indica varieties which shatter easily. Another explanation is that the use of the rather inefficient *ani-ani* knives is suited for sharing scarce employment opportunities in labor-surplus village societies.

The day of harvesting is made known by the paddy owner by installing a white flag in the rice fields. A group of harvesting workers consisting of mothers and daughters gather early in the morning in the fields with *ani-ani* knives in their hands, and at the signal, they begin cutting rice. The workers carry the harvested rice to the garden of the paddy owner to receive their fixed shares in kind, traditionally determined by the paddy owner, which range from one-ninth to one-sixth of the rice harvested. This system of rice harvesting is called *bawon*. The principle of mutual help in Javanese communal villages *(gotong-rojong)* has characterized this harvesting system and is a real example of the kind of "shared poverty" expounded by Professor Geertz.

This harvesting system, however, came into existence at a time when laborers were in rather short supply and population pressure was not very strong. Therefore the system had to face a big challenge with the growth in population as the supply of harvesting workers became redundant. According to one observation, five hundred workers poured into one hectare paddy field and took only one hour to finish their harvesting work. Naturally the share of rice earned by the workers declined to the range of one-eighteenth to one-twenty-second of the harvest. The harvesting workers would demand from the paddy owner an increase in their shares in order to survive. However, in the case of Java, even the paddy owner operated on dwarf-sized fields, and the increase of *bawon* in response to the workers' demand jeopardized the landowner's survival.

Because of the growing tension, the harvesting system had to be replaced and the new *tebasan* system spread rapidly. Under the *tebasan* system, paddy owners sold their standing crops to middlemen called *penebas* a few days before the harvest. The *penebas* organized the harvesting jobs on a commercial basis, which is different from the *bawon* system, in order to realize maximum profit from the sale of harvested rice. The *penebas* employed a fixed number of wage workers from within and outside villages instead of accepting free participation of harvesting workers which was practiced under the *bawon* system. Harvesting workers were asked to use sickles in order to reduce the harvesting costs (sickles are three to five times more efficient than the *ani-ani* knives). Furthermore, the *penebas* tended to employ the same workers continuously during one or more harvesting periods. Thus the employment opportunities of workers who had been freely participating in the harvesting work became smaller.

According to a survey, the number of workers needed to harvest four tons of unhulled rice per hectare was 184 persons under the *bawon* system, while the number of workers needed in the case of the *tebasan* system which made use of sickles was only 80 persons. The degradation of workers, who were excluded from participating in the harvesting work, became a serious matter. Several cases of protests from the workers against the restriction of labor participation in harvesting work under the *tebasan* system and the use of sickles in the place of the *ani-ani* knives were reported. However, in place of the patron-client relationship between the paddy owner and the harvesting workers, the relationship between the harvesting contractor and the hired workers began to emerge gradually but firmly. Although the number of hired workers was limited, their guaranteed period of employment was longer and their wages were higher than in the *bawon* system. According to a case study, the wage rate under the sickle-used *tebasan* system was about 73 percent higher than that in the *bawon* system. This fact has become a new force supporting the relationship between the harvesting contractor and the hired workers. Another important reason for sustaining the *tebasan* system is that the revenue of the paddy owner increased more under the *tebasan* system than in the *bawon* system. The average rate of revenue increase of the paddy owner under the *tebasan* system is about 20 percent. Consequently, the *tebasan* system has benefited both the harvesting contractor and the paddy owner, and the system has become more viable by internalizing a part of the harvesting workers into the *tebasan* system.

There is a case report which notes that the *bawon* system has been replaced by another system called *ceblokan* instead of the *tebasan* system. The *ceblokan* system does not limit the number of harvesting workers as does the *tebasan* system, but workers are required to provide additional services such as transplanting and weeding without payment in order to participate in harvesting work. Under the *ceblokan* system, wages of workers declined in real terms reflecting the decline in the bargaining power of the harvesting workers relative to the paddy owner. A survey conducted by Yujiro Hayami and Masao Kikuchi shows how the *bawon* system and *ceblokan* system have spread in West Java with the passage of time (Table 4.2). The survey indicates that the *bawon* system has changed gradually with a reduction in the number of harvesting workers, while the *ceblokan* system has changed to one in which the declining tendency of real wages has been intensified. The number of landless, idle workers, who being deprived of employment opportunities face starvation, has increased and a new order of villages that will alienate these workers from the community has emerged.

Although we have studied cases of Javanese villages in this chapter, the

Table 4.2

Rice Harvesting Systems in the South Subang Village (percentage of farmer adopters)

	BAWON				CEBLOKAN[a]					TOTAL
	PURELY OPEN	PPEN TO VILLAGES	OPEN WITH MAXIMUM LIMIT	LIMITED INVITEES	1/6 TRANS-PLANTING	1/7 TRANS-PLANTING	1/7 TRANS-PLANTING AND WEEDING	1/7 HARROWING AND TRANS-PLANTING	1/7 HARROWING, TRANS-PLANTING, AND WEEDING	
1950s	35	29	18	18						100
1960–61	29	3	21	19						100
1962–63	16	34	33	17						100
1964–65	9	16	16	32	27					100
1966–67	3	10	8	27	52					100
1968–69	1	4	6	19	44	24	2			100
1970–71			2	10	33	51	4			100
1972–73				8	17	67	8			100
1974–75				7	15	67	10	1		100
1976–77				4	7	67	18	2	2	100
1978				4		72	19	1	4	100

NOTE: a. 1/6 and 1/7 refer to harvesters' share.

SOURCE: Hayami, Y., and M. Kikuchi. 1981. *Asian Village Economy at the Crossroad: An Economic Approach to Institutional Change.* Tokyo: University of Tokyo Press.

same pattern of change in communal societies has been observed in other Southeast Asian villages. The population pressure, land subdivision, and the resulting polarization of peasantry is leading to a collapse of mutually helpful communal customs that have guaranteed the free and maximum participation of the labor of small-scale farmers and landless workers. There has been an accumulation of the poorest farmers on a large scale while the accommodative capacity of the poorest farmers under the traditional communal societies has been reduced. This phenomena can be properly described as the emergence of the "enclosure movement" in 20th century Asia.

According to the historical experience of the Western European countries, farmers who were pushed out of the villages were absorbed in the industrial labor force in the subsequent period. A serious problem for Southeast Asian countries is that such a process has not yet taken place due to the weak labor absorptive capacity of their industrialization process. Chapter 6 will discuss further the labor absorptive capacity of industrialization in Asia.

CHAPTER FIVE

The Mechanism of Agricultural Development

The Japanese Experience

Many Asian countries are under constant population pressure. Against this background, any improvement in the standard of living will require the vital task of increasing productivity through agricultural modernization.

How can this task of agricultural modernization in Asia be achieved? To answer this question, we can start by examining some Asian nations which have succeeded in agricultural modernization. We will first discuss the Japanese experience followed by the experiences of South Korea. Agricultural problems of other countries will be analyzed in comparison with the experiences of these two countries.

From the Japanese and South Korean experiences, it is very difficult to conclude that agricultural modernization originates from within the agricultural sector. Rather it is most likely that the agricultural sector increased its productivity in response to the impetus emanating from the nonagricultural sector, particularly from the industrial sector. The following two points are relevant in this respect. First, in the process of agricultural modernization, agricultural productivity can be improved only when modern agricultural inputs such as fertilizers, pesticides, agricultural machinery, and irrigation systems, are supplied in abundance. These inputs are all produced in the industrial sector. Moreover, agricultural productivity can be improved only when these modern agricultural inputs are supplied cheaply. Second, in order to break away from low-productivity agriculture, where a large number of farmers cultivate a small plot of land thereby resulting in low productivity per worker, surplus agricultural labor must be absorbed into the nonagricultural sector. Without doubt, in the case of Japan and South Korea, it was the industrial sector which absorbed the surplus agricultural labor.

These two conditions—namely, the supply of modern agricultural inputs required in the agricultural sector and the exhaustion of surplus agricultural labor—are indispensable factors for agricultural modernization and are created only by industrialization. It is not too much to say that it is almost impossible for agricultural modernization to occur in the heavily populated Asian countries unless industrialization proceeds at the same pace as agricultural development.

Let us elaborate this point further. As the surplus agricultural labor is withdrawn continuously from the agricultural sector in response to the demand for labor from the industrial sector, the number of farmers is reduced. At a certain point in time, with the tightening of the rural labor market, the agricultural wage will gradually begin to rise. At the same time, the agricultural sector is able to purchase agricultural inputs such as fertilizers and machinery cheaper than it did before because of the expansion of the industrial sector. As prices of these agricultural inputs decline and wages in the agricultural sector rise, there arises conditions for transformation from labor-intensive, low-productivity agriculture to high-productivity agriculture where modern agricultural inputs are used intensively. This chain of causation is summarized in Figure 5.1. If we look at the Japanese and South Korean experiences, agricultural modernization appears to have been achieved precisely as is depicted in the flow chart. Let us first discuss agricultural development in Japan. In Figure 5.2, which is based on data developed by Yujiro Hayami, the horizontal axis shows the rate of increase in prices of agricultural inputs and the vertical axis shows the rate of increase of inputs. Owing to a severe shortage of land, the rate of increase in land prices has remained high throughout the prewar and postwar periods and there has been little increase of land input. On the other hand, chemical fertilizers have been supplied in abundance at substantially reduced prices throughout both periods. As a result, the use of fertilizers has sharply increased and fertilizers have been substituted for land. By doing this, the productivity of scarce land has improved.

Nevertheless, production cannot be increased indefinitely by applying increased fertilizer to the traditional variety alone. Following the empirical law of diminishing returns, output per unit of land approaches the limit as the amount of fertilizer applications per unit of land increases (Figure 5.3). Because increased application of fertilizer inputs beyond f_1 does not contribute to an increase in output, it is essential that efforts are made to create a new variety, the so-called high-fertilizer, high-yielding improved variety, which will increase the quantity of output (q_2) in response to f_1 input of fertilizer.

The most important task of technological progress in Japanese agriculture, which had been severely constrained by the expansion of land, was precisely how to create a new variety characterized by high fertilizer use and high yields. Abolition of the feudalistic bindings by the Meiji Restoration in 1968 promoted farmers' organizations to freely open the seed exchange markets on a national scale. Through comparison of seed cultivation in various regions, high-fertilizers and high-yielding varieties such as "Shinriki," "Aikoku," and "Kame-no-O" were disseminated throughout the country. The spread of this technology, which is called "old farmers' technology" because it was brought about by well-experienced rich farmers, changed tra-

Figure 5.1 FLOW CHART OF AGRICULTURAL DEVELOPMENT

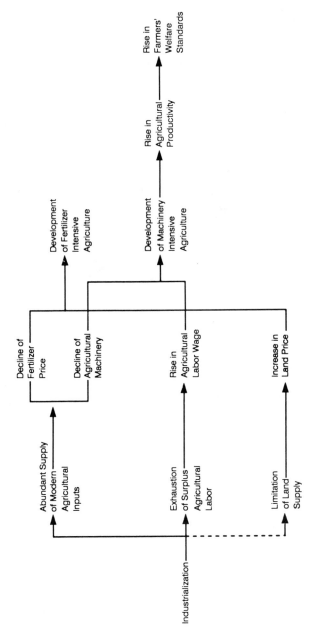

Figure 5.2 CHANGES IN PRICE AND INCREASED INPUTS OF AGRICULTURAL MATERIAL INPUTS IN JAPAN

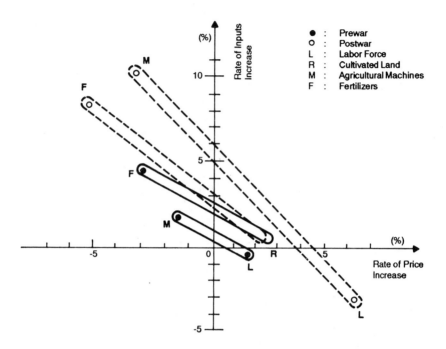

NOTES :   Prewar : Inputs 1880–1935, Prices 1890–1930
             Postwar : 1955–1965
             Prices   : Relative prices against the prices of agricultural products.

SOURCE :   Constructed from Hayami, Yujiro. 1973. *Nihon Nogyo no Seicho Katei [Growth
             process of the Japanese agriculture]*. Sobunsha: Tokyo.

ditional Japanese farming and revolutionalized the productivity of rice. In the Taisho era (1912–1926), however, as chemical fertilizers replaced natural fertilizers (for example, the replacement of soybean dregs imported from Manchuria with ammonium sulphate) and as cheap chemical fertilizers became available, more high-fertilizer high-yielding varieties were developed through the efforts of public agricultural experimental stations. Improved varieties such as "Rikuu 132," "Asahi 132," "Norin No. 1," and "Norin No. 8" began to spread before World War II. Through such efforts, yields per hectare of land in Japanese agriculture increased dramatically.

Let us go back to Figure 5.2 once again. In the postwar period, the labor shortage became a more serious problem than the scarcity of land. As a result, there were sharp increases in wages and various attempts were made

Figure 5.3 RELATIONSHIP BETWEEN YIELDS AND FERTILIZER INPUTS

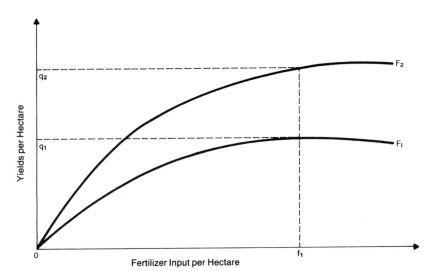

to save on labor. On the other hand, agricultural machinery was supplied abundantly at reduced prices as Japan strengthened its industrial capabilities. The process intensified the move to replace labor with machinery. As shown in Figure 5.2, labor input decreased as a result of an increase in the wage rate in the postwar period, while machinery input sharply increased due to the decline in the price of machinery. This is a clear indication that labor-saving or machinery-intensive agriculture was vigorously launched in the postwar period.

Through this development process, both land productivity (yield per hectare of land) and labor productivity (output per farmer) increased significantly. The increase in labor productivity in the postwar period was particularly remarkable. Indeed, as a result of the increase in labor productivity, the poverty-stricken rural area of Japan rapidly improved its standard of living in the postwar period.

South Korea's Compressed Process of Agricultural Development

Development of South Korean agriculture, which also achieved rapid modernization, followed a "compressed" pattern of the Japanese experience. Because labor absorption in South Korea's industrialization was strong (the industrialization of South Korea is discussed further in the next chapter), the farm population and the number of farm households began to decline in the late 1960s (Figure 5.4). This resulted in tight labor markets in the rural

Figure 5.4 TRENDS OF FARM POPULATION AND NUMBER OF FARM HOUSEHOLDS IN SOUTH KOREA

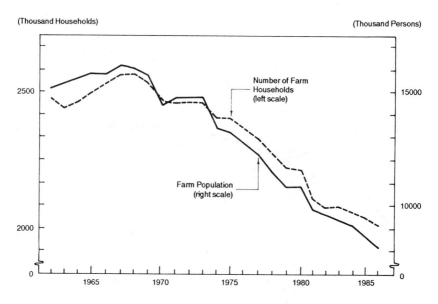

SOURCE :   Korea, Ministry of Agriculture and Fisheries. *Yearbook of Agriculture and Fisheries Statistics.* Seoul: MAF.

areas and an increase in wages (Figure 5.5A). A natural accompaniment to the economic development of South Korea, where room for hinterland development was very limited, was a rise in land prices. On the other hand, the industrialization process made the abundant and cheap supply of modern inputs such as fertilizers, pesticides, and machinery, possible. Because the price of chemical fertilizers, in particular, declined sharply and because of the extension of government credit for fertilizer purchases, the consumption of chemical fertilizers grew substantially in the 1970s. Thus, in South Korea, land prices and wage rates increased while prices of chemical fertilizers and agricultural machinery declined. This resulted in the more intensive use of cheaply available fertilizer in order to utilize expensive land more effectively and of cheaply available machinery in order to save on rising labor costs. As witnessed in Figure 5.5B, the land-to-capital and labor-to-capital ratios rose rapidly.

Consequently, both land productivity and labor productivity clearly began to rise (Figure 5.5C). The rate of increase in both land and labor productivity in Korea was faster than that of Japan which was one of the most successful in agricultural development. This is exactly what is meant when

Figure 5.5 INDICES OF SOUTH KOREAN AGRICULTURE

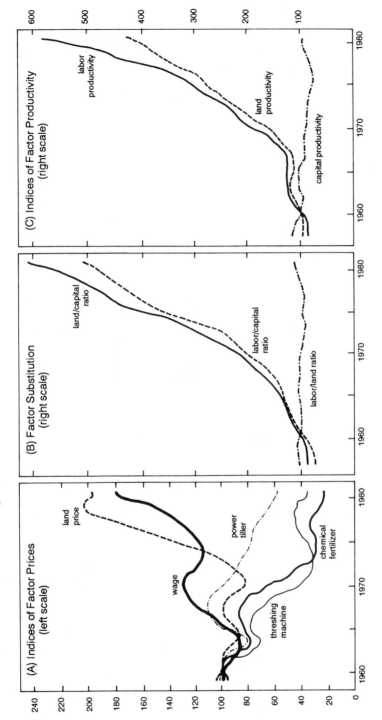

(A) Indices of Factor Prices (left scale)

land price

wage

power tiller

threshing machine

chemical fertilizer

(B) Factor Substitution (right scale)

land/capital ratio

labor/capital ratio

labor/land ratio

(C) Indices of Factor Productivity (right scale)

labor productivity

land productivity

capital productivity

SOURCE : Korea, Ministry of Agriculture and Fisheries. *Yearbook of Agriculture and Fisheries Statistics.* Seoul: MAF.

we say that South Korean agricultural development is a "compressed" version of the Japanese experience. As a result of the increase in labor productivity, farm household income, which was less than 60 percent of urban household income in the 1960s, began to rise rapidly. By the middle of the 1970s, urban and rural household incomes were almost at the same level (Figure 5.6).

We should, however, caution that the rise in South Korean agricultural productivity was realized not only because of the intensive use of fertilizers and agricultural machinery, but also because of efforts to introduce high-yielding varieties of rice. It was in 1965 when South Korea started to carry out research on a new variety as a national project. The Rural Development Agency was established in the same year and serious research and extension activities began. In 1969, a hybrid rice named "Unification" was developed at the request of South Korea by combining three rice varieties from Taiwan, Japan, and the International Rice Research Institute of the Philippines. This new variety of rice was planted at about ten thousand agricultural experimental stations throughout the country. After 1972, the operation to spread this Unification variety among farmers started, and it was greatly successful in both alleviating the food shortage and reducing imports. Aside from Unification, other new varieties were developed and disseminated. As of 1985, land productivity of rice in South Korea was the highest in Asia (Figure 5.7).

How We Interpret Southeast Asian Agriculture

In comparison with the South Korean experience, how should we interpret the process of agricultural development of the Southeast Asian countries? For Southeast Asian countries such as Indonesia and the Philippines, the shortage of land is as severe as in South Korea. As can be seen from Figure 5.8, the land input has ceased to increase since around 1970. However, the conditions to supply abundant and cheap chemical fertilizers exist in these countries as it did in the case of Korea. The chemical fertilizer industry in Indonesia was invigorated as a result of substantial increases in the price of oil. The self-sufficiency rate of the industry went up from 10 percent in the early 1970s to 100 percent in 1978, after which the industry has maintained a sizeable export potential. Although the self-sufficiency rate of the chemical fertilizer industry in the Philippines has been low, owing partly to the problem of supply of raw materials, the supply price has continuously declined through imports from Indonesia, South Korea, and Taiwan.

As can be seen from Figure 5.9, the increase in fertilizer inputs in Indonesia and the Philippines was higher than in South Korea. As was discussed in Chapter 3, fertilizer-responsive HYVs had already been introduced in Southeast Asia, and there is no doubt that the productivity of agricultural

Figure 5.6 FARM HOUSEHOLD INCOME (Yr) AND URBAN FARM HOUSEHOLD INCOME (Yu) IN SOUTH KOREA

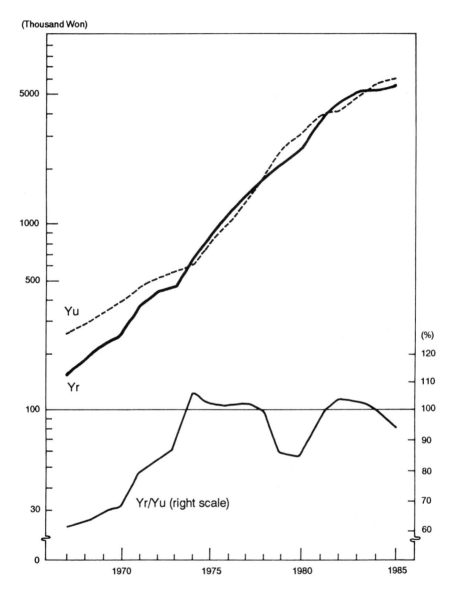

SOURCES :   Korea, Economic Planning Board. *Annual Report of the Family Income and Expenditure Survey.* Seoul: EPB; Korea, Ministry of Agriculture and Fisheries. *Report on the Results of Farm Household Economy Survey and Production Cost Survey of Agricultural Products.* Seoul: MAF.

Figure 5.7 RICE YIELDS IN SELECTED ASIAN COUNTRIES, 1985

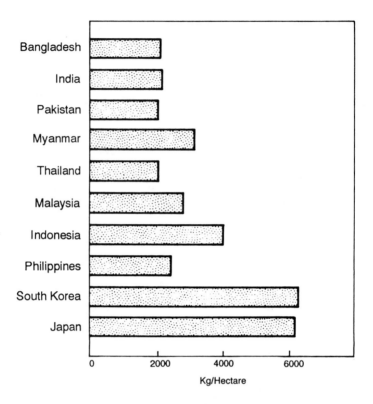

SOURCE :   Food and Agriculture Organization. *Production Yearbook*. Rome: FAO.

land in Southeast Asia increased at a considerable speed, if not at the same speed as that of South Korea. If we look at Figure 5.10, however, the rapidly increasing trend of labor input is still sustained in heavily populated South-east Asia. As a matter of fact, labor inputs in Indonesia and the Philippines have accelerated in the 1970s. Therefore, it is difficult to expect increases in labor productivity.

While the labor productivity of South Korea improved by 4.4 percent per annum during the period, in Southeast Asia, improvement was only 1.6 per-cent for the Philippines and 1.3 percent for Indonesia. Increases in labor pro-ductivity, which is expressed as productivity of land multiplied by land input per unit of labor, is possible either through the increase in land productivity and/or increase in land input per unit of labor. The average annual rates of increase (G) in labor productivity, land productivity, and land input per unit

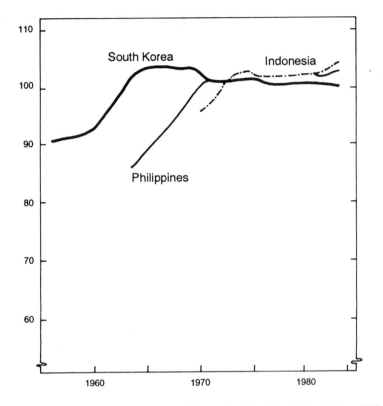

Figure 5.8 INDICES OF LAND INPUTS IN SELECTED
ASIAN COUNTRIES

(1976 = 100 : 3-Year Moving Average)

SOURCE : Food and Agriculture Organization. *Production Yearbook*. Rome: FAO.

of labor for the three countries during each observed period are shown in Table 5.1.

Despite the shortage of land, land input per unit of labor has not decreased in the case of South Korean agriculture owing to the massive labor migration from the rural area in response to labor absorption in the industrial sector. Therefore, the increase in labor productivity in South Korea has been totally due to an increase in land productivity. In contrast, although land productivity increased in the Philippines and Indonesia, about one-half of the increase was lost by the decrease in land per farmer; as a result, these countries experienced only a modest rise in labor productivity.

A rapid rise in land productivity in the Southeast Asian countries that is

Figure 5.9 INDICES OF FERTILIZER INPUTS IN SELECTED ASIAN COUNTRIES

(1976 = 100 : 3-Year Moving Average)

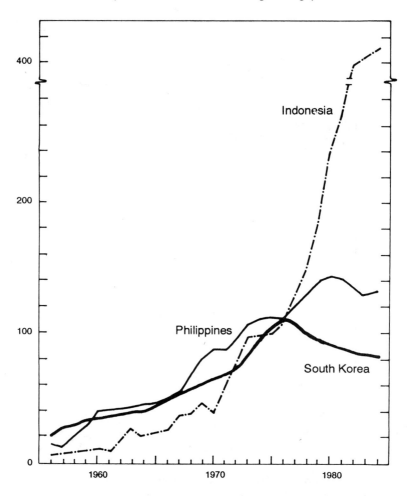

SOURCE :   Food and Agriculture Organization. *Fertilizer Yearbook*. Rome: FAO.

Figure 5.10 INDICES OF LABOR INPUTS IN SELECTED ASIAN COUNTRIES

(1976 = 100 : 3-Year Moving Average)

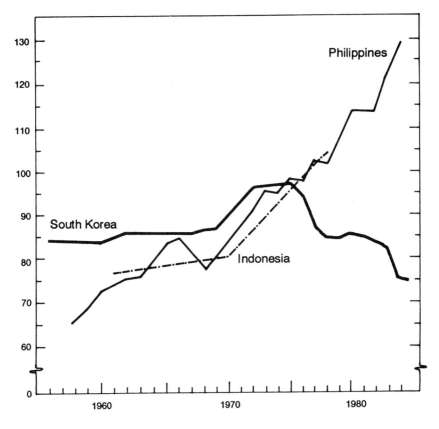

SOURCES :   Korea, Ministry of Agriculture and Fisheries. *Yearbook of Agriculture and Fisheries Statistics.* Seoul: MAF; Philippines, Central Bank. *Statistical Bulletin.* Manila: CB; Indonesia. Population censuses.

associated with the introduction of HYVs is obviously a new trend to watch. However, the limited boundaries of cultivable land coupled with the trend of a growing labor force have been adversely affecting these countries. Thus, improvement in labor productivity and welfare levels in Southeast Asian countries continues to be a difficult task to overcome.

Table 5.1
Agricultural Productivity of Selected Asian Countries

COUNTRY	G(Q/L)	=	G(Q/R)	−	G(R/L)
Indonesia	1.3%	=	2.8%	−	1.5%
Philippines	1.6%	=	3.0%	−	1.4%
South Korea	4.4%	=	4.5%	−	0.1%

NOTES: Q = agricultural output
   R = area of cultivated land
   L = labor force
   Q/L = labor productivity (output per unit of labor)
   Q/R = land productivity (output per unit of cultivated land)
   R/L = land-labor ratio (cultivated land per unit of labor)
   Q/L = Q/R × R/L

CHAPTER SIX

Strategies for Industrialization

Initial Conditions for Industrialization

In the previous chapter, a mechanism through which industrialization brought about agricultural modernization in the developing countries of Asia was discussed. However, industrialization itself has not been discussed in this book thus far. The subject of how industrialization can be realized is extremely important for the developing countries as a whole rather than for the Asian countries alone. In fact, ever since independence from the colonial powers, all of the developing countries have been keenly searching for economic modernization through industrialization. They have always placed great hope on industrialization as the best tool for economic modernization. Thus, this chapter deals with questions such as: What strategies were adopted in Asian countries in realizing industrialization? What were the results? What problems are left to be resolved?

A major premise in discussing industrialization in Asia is that most countries were formerly under a colonial rule imposed by either Japan or the Western countries. Consequently, industrialization in the developing Asian countries began with an economic structure that had been distorted by the colonial rule. In other words, the initial conditions these countries faced in their drive for industrialization was the economic structure of the colonial period. What then was the basic characteristic of a colony? The colony was an area that had been developed using the capital and technology of the home country in order to supply the home country with certain food items and industrial raw materials. This structure of a colonial economy is characterized by the term "monoculture economy." In this section, the case of Malaysia, which was once a typical British colony in Asia, is examined.

The most prominent feature of the Malaysian economy has been its structure of a monoculture economy. Under long British colonial rule, the Malaysian economy produced a few export-oriented primary products such as tin and natural rubber. When the British colonial rule over Malaysia finally ended in 1957, there were virtually no established industries other than tin mining and rubber planting. As can be seen from Figure 6.1, the two major export products—tin and natural rubber—had particularly high export shares during the early 1960s (however, their shares have decreased in recent years due to increased efforts in exporting manufactured products). Like

Figure 6.1 SHARE OF PRIMARY PRODUCTS IN TOTAL EXPORTS OF MALAYSIA

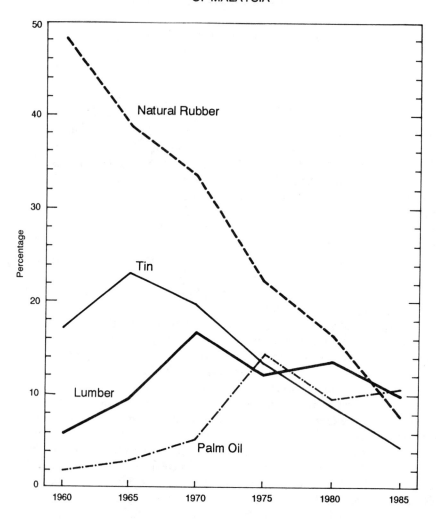

SOURCE :   Bank Negara Malaysia. *Quarterly Economic Bulletin.* Kuala: Bank Negara Malaysia.

Malaysia, most Asian countries had a distorted economic structure under colonial rule which greatly depended upon the production of export-oriented primary commodities. Inevitably, industrialization made very little progress since domestic demand for industrial goods was met by imports from the colonial home country. In other words, the majority of Asian countries were "dependent" economies which prospered only from the demand of the home country for their primary products. Under these circumstances, what strategies were available for these Asian countries to start industrialization?

One possible strategy for a monoculture country striving for industrialization is to, first, effectively utilize its resources under the initial conditions. Through exports of primary products, the country would be able to obtain the foreign exchange it needed to purchase the basic requirements for industrialization including technology, parts and other intermediate goods, and machines and equipment from the developed countries. This option, which may be called an "industrialization through primary exports" strategy, was once adopted by the United States and Canada which were themselves initially monoculture countries. However, the Asian countries did not employ this strategy. Although they had abundant resources for production of primary commodities, the export markets for their products after World War II did not provide a favorable environment for producers. At the time of the war, rapid technological progress in the developed countries made possible the abundant supply of synthetics and substitutes for primary products. The world economy became less dependent on the primary products exported from Asian countries. For instance, natural rubber and fiber were increasingly replaced by synthetics. Plastics were widely used as substitutes for tinware and wooden products. Furthermore, the developed countries generally took a strong protectionist policy in trying to preserve their domestic agriculture and to increase their rate of self-sufficiency in food. Therefore, the volume of primary products exported from the developing countries remained stagnant and prices of primary products remained at low levels. Inevitably, the Asian countries did not opt for the strategy of industrialization through exporting primary products.

Protectionist Pattern of Industrialization

The second strategy for industrialization was that of a protectionist type. This strategy was in fact the one that was adopted by the majority of the Asian countries. It is natural to launch an inward-looking industrialization aimed at protecting the domestic market when a country is unable to adopt the strategy of industrialization through primary exports. This protectionist pattern of industrialization is called import-substituting industrialization.

With this strategy, the volume of imports is controlled by a high tariff barrier, an import quota, or other restrictive measures. Then, domestic products gradually substitute for the imported goods through increased production within the country to fill the vacuum in the market.

In Figure 6.2, developing country A is now importing manufactured goods, say automobiles, from developed country B without any import duty or quantitative restriction. Under this situation, it would not pay for country A to produce automobiles domestically since imported cars are of better quality and can be obtained at a lower price. The shaded portion in the figure represents the domestic car market in country A. Thus, as long as country A freely imports cars from country B, the entire market is filled with imported cars. If, however, country A closes its doors to imported cars by setting up a high tariff barrier or by adopting a quantitative restriction policy, there will be a vacuum in the domestic market that was formerly satisfied by the imported cars. Domestic entrepreneurs will then be able to produce cars to fill this vacuum. As this process is successfully undertaken, country A will be able to make an advance in its industrialization with the domestically produced goods substituting for imports. This is what is called the process of import-substituting industrialization.

However, country A still must depend on the imported parts, intermediate goods, and assembly machines for domestic car production, since it cannot produce these goods domestically at the initial stages of industrialization

Figure 6.2 CONCEPTUALIZED CHART OF
IMPORT-SUBSTITUTING INDUSTRIALIZATION

Country B

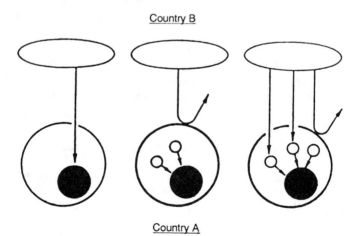

Country A

due to its weak industrial base. The usual process was to assemble cars domestically using imported parts, intermediate goods, and machines and equipment, and sell the cars as the final products in the domestic market. In Asia, it was also intended that the previously imported parts and machinery would be gradually substituted by domestic-made products as the industrial base strengthened.

In the case of Thailand, the share of consumer goods in the total amount of imports declined significantly from about 30 percent in the mid-1960s to 10 percent in the mid-1970s (Figure 6.3). This reflects the fact that during this period, import substitution in consumer goods made rapid progress in Thailand. In contrast, it can be seen that the share of imported parts and intermediate goods required for the domestic production of consumer goods increased rapidly during the same period. Thailand has continuously undertaken import-substituting industrialization through domestic production of consumer goods using imported capital goods to assemble and process the input materials that were also imported from abroad.

As the promoters of industrialization, entrepreneurs in Asian countries had not grown in sufficient numbers under the long colonial rule. The shortage of domestic entrepreneurs was a major obstacle to progress in import-substituting industrialization. Inevitably, foreign companies had to be invited from the developed countries in order to make progress in indus-

Figure 6.3 IMPORT SUBSTITUTION OF CONSUMER GOODS IN THAILAND

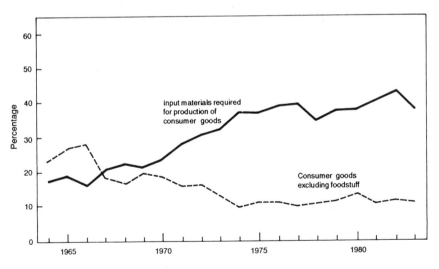

SOURCE :   United Nations, Economic and Social Commission for Asia and the Pacific.
             Statistical Yearbook for Asia and the Pacific. Bangkok: ESCAP.

trialization. It can be said that import-substituting industrialization in Asian countries has been largely promoted by joint ventures between local enterprises and foreign private companies. Among the local enterprises, the most capable ones for joint ventures in many Asian countries have been the Chinese-owned companies. In short, the promoters of industrialization in Asian countries have been the joint ventures between the Chinese-owned local enterprises and the subsidiaries of multinational companies.

Companies of the developed countries had good reason to launch their operations in Asian countries. At that time, most Asian countries had adopted policies of strict import control in order to promote their import-substituting industrialization. As a result, it had become difficult for goods produced by companies of the developed countries to enter into the Asian market through ordinary forms of trade. Thus, the developed-country firms actively started their operations in import-substituting sectors of the Asian countries so that they could regain the shares of the market that they formerly held through their exports. This kind of activity matched well with the industrial policies of Asian countries in that the companies were able to become involved in industrial production in a noncompetitive environment created by the protectionist policies of the Asian countries. Furthermore, the governments of the Asian countries provided incentives for foreign companies which were in harmony with their policies of import-substituting industrialization. They offered generous privileges particularly to the companies of "pioneer industries" for which local capital and technology were still unavailable. Thus, companies of the developed countries could regain local markets of Asian countries from which they had been excluded due to the policies of import-substituting industrialization. It follows that their operations soon became large-scale under a very privileged industrial environment.

Industrialization in the Southeast Asian countries initially made great advances through import substitution. As can be seen from Figure 6.4, the share of the manufacturing industry in GDP in these countries has been increasing at a high rate. In the Philippines, which used to be a colony of the United States, American companies were significant even after independence. Furthermore, the Philippine government offered the same privileges to the Americans as those given to local companies. Since most of the domestic capital in the Philippines was concentrated in a few conglomerates, import-substituting industrialization was promoted by joint venture enterprises between these local conglomerates and American companies as early as the mid-1950s. In this respect, the Philippines was ahead of other Asian countries. Thailand had an economic boom until the mid-1960s with a sizeable inflow of foreign capital that was associated with the demand for special procurement during the Vietnam War. Import-substituting industrialization in Thailand was, therefore, mainly promoted by foreign private companies. It was the first attempt at industrialization in the country, which had not possessed a well-established industrial sector since it started as a rice monoculture in the mid-19th century. Industrialization was also launched through import-substitution in the 1960s in Malaysia, where, as a typical monoculture, its economic structure was extremely biased toward production of tin and natural rubber. Textiles and electric machineries were the major sectors where foreign companies promoted import substitution. These events were epochal for many Asian countries which had not experienced full-fledged industrialization under colonial rule.

Weak Labor Absorptive Capacity

Today's high rate of industrialization in the Asian countries could not have been achieved if the strategy of import-substituting industrialization had not been adopted. Thus, this strategy was of great value to those countries. However, this strategy had many problems as well; the most important problem for the purposes of this book is the fact that the labor absorptive capacity of this strategy was very weak. In fact, this has been a serious obstacle to progress in agricultural modernization and has resulted in the accumulation of the urban poor, which is the topic to be discussed in the next chapter.

It seems appropriate at this point to briefly look at the degree of labor absorption attained by industrialization in some Asian countries. It is widely known that in the Asian NIEs, there was tremendous advancement in industrialization (industrialization in the NIES will be taken up again in Chapter 8). However, as we saw in Figure 6.4, the share of the manufacturing industry increased in the Southeast Asian countries as well. The share of the industrial sector—broadly defined to include mining, manufacturing, construction, and utilities—to GDP or "the rate of industrialization" in general has been as high in the Southeast Asian countries as it has in the NIEs. For example, the rate of industrialization of the Philippines, Malaysia, and Indonesia are almost as high as the rates for South Korea and Taiwan (Figure 6.5).

In Asian NIEs such as South Korea and Taiwan, a rapid increase in the rate of industrialization in production was accompanied by a concurrent increase in the rate of industrialization in employment. In the case of the Southeast Asian countries, however, an increase in the rate of industrialization in employment did not correspond with an increase in the rate of industrialization in production. This trend is shown in Figure 6.5 which shows the changes in the rate of industrialization in employment together with the rate of industrialization in production for five different years between 1960

Figure 6.4 SHARE OF THE MANUFACTURING INDUSTRY IN SOUTHEAST ASIAN COUNTRIES[a]

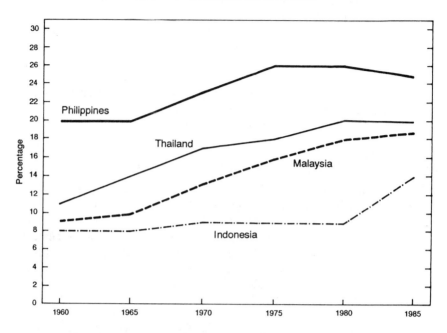

NOTE :   a. (manufacturing output/GDP) ×[RT] 100

SOURCE :   World Bank. *World Development Report.* New York: WB.

and 1980 (the rate of industrialization in employment is defined here as the share of industrial workers in the total labor force employed). It can be inferred that the pattern of industrialization in Southeast Asia was a labor-saving one, while the pattern in the Asian NIEs was labor absorptive.

Why did labor-saving industrialization occur in the Southeast Asian countries where there was abundant labor? As has been noted, industrialization in the Southeast Asian countries was achieved through a protectionist approach of import substitution where industrialization is achieved through the production of goods for the domestic market while an import control policy shut out imported goods. Only parts, intermediate goods, machines, and equipment required for import-substituting production were imported from the developed countries. (In fact, a favorable exchange rate and lower import duties were also often applied to ease import of these input materials.) However, these imported machines and equipment were originally designed to be labor-saving, reflecting the situation of labor shortage in the developed countries. In addition, since industrialization in the Southeast

Figure 6.5 THE RATE OF INDUSTRIALIZATION IN PRODUCTION AND IN EMPLOYMENT IN ASIA

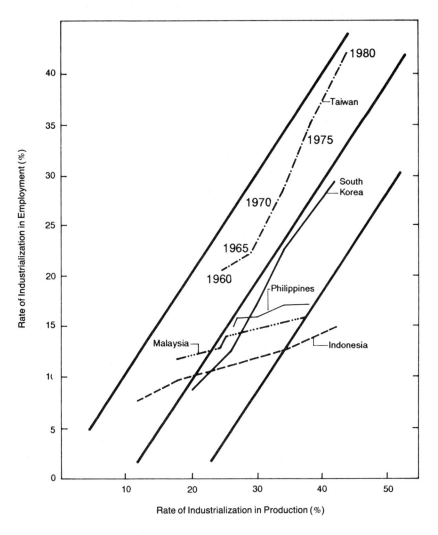

NOTE :   Diagonals indicate cases where industrialization progresses at the same rate both in employment and in production.

SOURCE :   World Bank. *World Tables, Third Edition,* vol. I, II. New York: WB.

Asian countries was mainly promoted by joint ventures between local enterprises and the subsidiaries of the multinational companies based in the
developed countries, it was natural for those subsidiaries to introduce the
labor-saving type of technology owned by their parent companies. Thus, the
form of industrial production in Southeast Asian countries became one
which could not absorb the abundant labor force.

It is usually costly for foreign companies to create a labor-intensive type of
technology which conforms to local conditions. This is reflected in the fact
that the typical import-substituting industry launched by the foreign companies was the car assembly industry. The efficiency of an assembly plant in a
developed country depends upon the technical efficiency of its production
management of machine parts. Thus, to isolate and transfer the assembly
portion of production to another country does not damage the efficiency of
the production system of the industry as a whole. However, because machine
parts of good quality could not be produced locally in the Southeast Asian
countries, the import-substituting assembly industry that had been set up
with foreign capital needed to import the input materials from the developed countries. The industry, therefore, was constrained by the technological environment of the developed countries. Thus, almost all of the car
assembly plants in the Southeast Asian countries—to repeat again, a typical
example of an import-substituting industry in the region—are "branch factories" of foreign companies. Production technology and the assembly section are totally controlled by the parent companies. It was inevitable that the
process of import substitution in Southeast Asian countries should become
more capital-intensive due to the strong influence of the technological environment of the parent companies which were located in the developed countries. Accordingly, these import-substituting industries had only a weak
labor absorptive capacity.

In contrast, the labor absorptive capacity of industrialization in South
Korea and Taiwan was noticeably strong (Figure 6.5). What was the reason
behind this? Unlike the Southeast Asian countries, the Asian NIES did not
undertake import-substituting industrialization but adopted the strategy of
export-oriented industrialization. South Korea and Taiwan launched a vigorous export drive to expand their industrial goods market in the mid-1960s.
The governments offered various incentives to the export industries including subsidies, reduction or exemption of corporate income taxes, and a large
amount of export finance. Due to their policy of export promotion, the production of industrial goods increased significantly in South Korea and Taiwan. Among others, production of labor-intensive goods such as textiles,
plywood, and sundry goods rapidly increased.

Supported by the high rate of economic growth in the developed countries, the demand for these products has been continuously increasing at a

high rate. A rapid increase in demand started in the mid-1960s when South Korea and Taiwan launched their export-oriented industrialization and continued until the first oil crisis in the mid-1970s. The international environment was indeed favorable for the export of industrial goods from the Asian NIEs. In addition, the developed countries went through a turbulent structural change during this period. A large number of rapidly growing industries emerged one after another in the process of high economic growth while many other industries declined. The majority of declining industries in the developed countries were labor-intensive ones such as textiles, which lost competitiveness due to an upward trend in wages. As a result, the Asian NIEs were able to penetrate into the depths of the market for such labor-intensive goods in the developed countries.

Let us look at how far labor-intensive goods contributed to the promotion of the export-oriented industrialization strategy in the Asian NIEs by taking South Korea in the 1970s (when this strategy was most actively undertaken) as an example. Table 6.1 shows in descending order the value of exports of the manufacturing industries in South Korea. The top three industries—

Table 6.1
Indices for Manufactured Exports of South Korea, 1970

MANUFACTURING INDUSTRY	VALUE OF EXPORTS ($1,000)	LABOR COEFFICIENT[a]	RELATIVE WAGE[b]
Apparels	232,530	0.35	0.67
Sundry goods	119,499	0.35	0.80
Lumber, plywood and furniture	96,596	0.32	0.74
Cotton yarn	50,904	0.18	0.76
Textiles	46,772	0.31	0.76
Electric machines	4,637	0.19	1.03
Food processing	44,634	0.20	1.09
Rubber products	18,016	0.28	0.75
Metal products	12,781	0.33	0.91
Steel products	9,901	0.16	1.36
Transport machines	9,645	0.15	1.41
Machinery	7,923	0.33	0.94
Other chemical products	7,578	0.13	1.29
Nonferrous mining products	6,651	0.23	1.22
Chemical fertilizers	6,333	0.05	1.15
Nonferrous metals	5,627	0.12	1.13
All manufacturing industries	737,182	0.20	1.00

NOTES: a. Defined as l(L/Y) where L = number of laborers and Y = production value.
b. Defined as w(W$_i$/W) where W$_i$ = wage for the ith manufacturing industry and W = average wage for all manufacturing industries.

SOURCE: Economic Planning Board. 1971. *Korea Statistical Yearbook*. Seoul: EPB.

Table 6.2

Labor Absorption of Manufactured Exports in Selected Asian Countries

	SOUTH KOREA	TAIWAN	THAILAND	PHILIPPINES	JAPAN
Employment induced by exports (1,000)	886	511	150	129	2,265
Total employment (1,000)	2,107	1,501	1,356	1,326	14,364
Export-induced employment as a share of total employment (%)	42.05	34.04	11.06	9.73	15.77

SOURCE: Institute of Developing Economies. 1982. *International Input-Output Table for ASEAN Countries 1975*. Tokyo: IDE.

namely, clothing, wooden products, and sundry goods—should be noted. The total amount of exports from these three industries constituted more than 60 percent of total exports of manufacturing industries in 1970. At the same time, the coefficients of labor intensiveness for these industries (i.e., the number of workers in the sector divided by the total amount of production) were among the highest of all manufacturing industries. The table also shows the relative wage level of each industry with the average wage of all the industries as 1.00. It can be seen that the three industries noted are typical low-wage sectors. Thus, the industrial sectors which promoted economic growth in South Korea were the export sectors of labor-intensive industries. These industries naturally had a strong labor absorptive capacity and best fitted the labor surplus situation in South Korea at that time. Table 6.2, which shows the percentage of employment induced by the export of manufactured goods, indicates that exports actually created 30–40 percent of total manufacturing employment in South Korea and Taiwan.

In the case of the Southeast Asian countries, the demand for labor in the industrial sector has been small despite the abundant supply of labor arising from the continuously high rate of population growth. This is again in contrast to South Korea and Taiwan where the rate of increase in population and labor force has been gradually declining. Therefore, the Southeast Asian countries are faced with difficulties in absorbing a surplus of agricultural labor force, which in turn slows down the process of agricultural modernization. Weak labor absorption of the industrial sector is also an important factor in the accumulation of the urban poor. This subject will be discussed in the next chapter.

CHAPTER SEVEN

Urbanization in Agony

The Mobility Revolution

In Asian countries, the urbanization rate (i.e., the ratio of the urban population to the total population) has been increasing at an extremely high rate. The rate of increase in the urban population far exceeds the rate of increase in urban employment. Hence, the provisions of social overhead capital such as housing, school, and health facilities cannot cope with the rapidly increasing population in the cities.

This phenomenon is called "overurbanization." Overurbanization is reflected in the existence of extensive slum areas in Southeast Asian cities. The ratio of the population living in slum areas is particularly high in the principal city of each country. It is estimated that the ratio of the slum population to the total population in the city reaches 20 percent in Metro-Bangkok, 26 percent in Jakarta, and 35 percent in the Manila Metropolitan Area. This chapter looks at the distorted pattern of urbanization in Asian countries and examines the reasons behind it.

The increase in urban population is partly due to a natural increase in the population (i.e., the number of births minus deaths). However, a notably large portion of the increase is caused by a migration of the rural population into the city. People are continuously coming into the city even though the demand for labor in the urban industrial sector is small. Thus, the majority of new migrants are compelled to work in a services sector called the "urban informal sector." The urban informal sector is composed of such trivial jobs as street vendors, peddlers, repairmen, shop assistants, and day laborers. The prominent feature of this sector is the ease of entry. Only a trifling amount of initial capital is needed to start a business in this sector, and jobs do not require a high level of skills. Accordingly, the migrant population tends to be concentrated in the urban informal sector, and further pushes down this sector's already low productivity and low wages. The situation of underemployment in the sector is also worsening.

The ILO's report on Kenya published in 1972 was the first to take a closer look at the existence of the urban informal sector for the first time. According to the report, the said sector is defined as having the following pre-requisites; (1) ease of entry, (2) reliance on indigenous resources, (3) family ownership of enterprises, (4) small scale of operation, (5) labor-intensive and adapted technology,

(6) skills acquired outside the formal school system, and (7) unregulated and competitive markets. In short, it can be concluded that the entry into the informal sector is easier than other sectors because of the factors from (2) to (7) listed above. (ILO. 1972. *Employment, Income and Equity: A Strategy for Increasing Productive Employment in Kenya*. Geneva: ILO)

The urban informal sector is an essential source of livelihood for the urban poor. Recognizing this, the World Bank, the ILO, and others have recently been pursuing active research in this sector. Based on the findings of these research efforts, the ratio of workers in the urban informal sector to the total labor force were found to be high in general in the major cities of Asia (Table 7.1).

In Table 7.2, the rates of increase of the urban and total population in Asian countries during the first half of the 1980s are compared. Despite some differences between the countries, the rate of increase in the urban population is always higher than that of the total population. Such a rate of increase in the urban population cannot be explained by natural increase alone. It seems that a social increase, which is caused by an influx of population from the rural area, accounts for a major portion of the increase. It is necessary to look at the demographic statistics in order to analyze mobility patterns; unfortunately the statistics are not available in many Asian countries. For the sake of convenience, it is simply assumed that the rate of social increase in the urban population is equivalent to the rate of increase in the urban population minus that of the total population. Assuming this, the fourth column in Table 7.2 is equal to the rate of social increase in urban population during the early 1980s. The ratio of the rate of social increase to

Table 7.1

Ratio of Workers in the Urban Informal Sector
to Total Labor Force in Selected Asian Countries
(percentage)

COUNTRY	CITY	WORKERS IN INFORMAL SECTOR
India	Calcutta	40–50
	Ahmadabad	47
Indonesia	Jakarta	45
Malaysia	All cities in West Malaysia	35
Pakistan	All cities	69
Sri Lanka	Colombo	19
Thailand	All cities	26

SOURCE: Sethuraman, S. V., ed. 1981. *The Urban Informal Sector in Developing Countries: Employment, Poverty and Environment*. Geneva: ILO.

Table 7.2

Rate of Increase in Urban Population in Selected Asian Countries,
1980–1985 (percentage)

COUNTRY	RATE OF INCREASE IN URBAN POPULATION	RATE OF INCREASE IN TOTAL POPULATION	RATE OF SOCIAL INCREASE IN URBAN POPULATION
Bangladesh	7.9	2.6	5.3
India	3.9	2.2	1.7
Indonesia	2.3	2.1	0.2
Malaysia	4.0	2.5	1.5
Myanmar (Burma)	2.8	1.9	0.9
Pakistan	4.8	2.7	2.1
Philippines	3.2	2.5	0.7
Thailand	3.2	2.1	1.1

SOURCE: United Nations. *Demographic Yearbook*. New York: UN.

Table 7.3

Social Increase of Urban Population in Selected
Asian Countries

COUNTRY	RATIO OF SOCIAL INCREASE TO TOTAL INCREASE IN URBAN POPULATION	
	1965–1980	1980–1985
Bangladesh	66	67
India	36	44
Indonesia	51	9
Malaysia	44	38
Myanmar (Burma)	21	44
Pakistan	28	44
Philippines	30	22
Thailand	41	34

SOURCE: United Nations. *Demographic Yearbook*. New York:
UN.

the rate of total increase in urban population is shown in Table 7.3. It can be
seen from the table that, in general, an influx of population from rural areas
has contributed significantly to urbanization in Asian countries since 1965.
Professors A. Rogers and J. G. Williamson paid special attention to the fact
that the population explosion in Asian cities was being caused by a rural-
urban migration and called this phenomenon the "mobility revolution."

The rate of increase in the urban population is particularly high in large
cities. From Table 7.4, which shows the average annual rate of increase in the

Table 7.4
Average Annual Rate of Increase in Urban Population in Selected Principal
Cities of Asia (percentage)

COUNTRY	PRINCIPAL CITY	PERIOD	AVERAGE ANNUAL RATE OF INCREASE IN POPULATION
Bangladesh	Dacca	1961–1974	10.2
India	Calcutta	1961–1971	5.5
Indonesia	Jakarta	1961–1971	5.2
Pakistan	Karachi	1961–1972	6.1
Philippines	Manila	1960–1970	5.5
Thailand	Bangkok	1960–1970	5.5

SOURCES: Country population censuses.

urban population between two recent censuses in the principal cities of Asia, it can be seen that the rate of increase in the population of the principal city far exceeds the rate of increase in the total urban population. Thus, urbanization in Asian countries may be called the process of "metropolitanization."

Interindustry Mobility of Labor

The experiences of Japan and the Western countries show that the center of production activities is always located in the city and the core of such activities is the industrial sector. In these countries, the rapidly expanding urban industrial sector induced a strong demand for labor and brought about an increase in wages which, in turn, pulled the rural population into the city.

In the Asian countries, however, this traditional pattern of interindustry mobility of labor, wherein the labor force migrating out of the agricultural sector is absorbed into the industrial sector, can be found only in the Asian NIEs such as South Korea and Taiwan. Other Asian countries did not experience such a pattern of labor mobility. Instead, only a small portion of the labor force flowing out of agriculture has been absorbed in the industrial sector, and the majority of the migrating labor force has been entering into the traditional services sector. While it would be appropriate to examine this further, official data on the interindustry mobility of labor are not available in the Asian countries. It is, therefore, assumed that the index of interindustry mobility of labor is equivalent to the rate of increase in the labor force in a specific industry minus the rate of increase in the total labor force in all industries. If the index is positive, it can be said that there has been a positive inflow of labor from other sectors to the sector concerned. If the index is negative, then the labor force has migrated out of the sector to other sectors. As shown in Table 7.5, there is a marked contrast between the labor mobility experiences of the Asian NIEs and the Southeast Asian countries. Although migration of labor from agriculture to other sectors can be found in all four countries, the indexes are particularly high for South Korea and Taiwan. For both these cases, the rate of labor inflow into the industrial sector is significantly high, exceeding the rate of labor inflow into the services sector. On the other hand, in the case of Indonesia and the Philippines, the rate of labor outflow from the agricultural sector, though it continuously exists, has been low. The rate of inflow into the industrial sector has not been high and was even negative for the Philippines. In other words, the labor force has been migrating out of the industrial sector in the Philippines. The labor force flowing out of both the agricultural and the industrial sectors has been concentrated in the services sector. The highest rate of labor inflow has also been noted in the services sector in Indonesia.

If we assume that all labor migrating out of the agricultural sector enter into other sectors, it is possible to obtain a rough estimate of the proportion of the ex-agricultural labor force that entered into the respective industries (Table 7.6). In South Korea and Taiwan, 65–75 percent of the ex-agricultural labor force is concentrated in the industrial sector. However, the percentage is lower in Indonesia and the Philippines. The rate of inflow into the services sector is 25–35 percent in South Korea and Taiwan, while it is significantly high at 74 percent and 131 percent in Indonesia and the Philippines, respectively.

Table 7.5

Index of Interindustry Mobility of Labor in Selected Asian Countries
(percentage)

COUNTRY	$G(L_A)$–$G(L)$	$G(L_I)$–$G(L)$	$G(L_S)$–$G(L)$
Indonesia (1971–1980)	−1.97	2.62	<3.02
Philippines (1960–1980)	−0.89	−0.79	<1.80
South Korea (1963–1980)	−3.61	6.70	>2.40
Taiwan (1960–1980)	−4.25	3.85	>1.17

NOTES: $G(L_A)$ = rate of increase in the agricultural labor force
  $G(L_I)$ = rate of increase in the industrial labor force
  $G(L_S)$ = rate of increase in the services labor force
  $G(L)$ = rate of increase in the total labor force

SOURCES: South Korea, Economic Planning Board. *Annual Report on the Economically Active Population Survey.* Seoul: EPB; Taiwan, Directorate General of Budget, Accounting and Statistics. *Yearbook of Labor Statistics.* Taipei: DGBAS; Philippines, National Economic Development Authority. *Yearbook of Labor Statistics.* Manila: NEDA; Indonesia, Biro Pusat Statistik. *Indikator Ekonomi.* Jakarta: BPS.

Table 7.6
Sectoral Share of Labor Force Out-Migrating from the Agricultural Sector
in Selected Asian Countries (percentage)

COUNTRY	INFLOW INTO THE INDUSTRIAL SECTOR	INFLOW INTO THE SERVICES SECTOR
Indonesia (1971–1980)	25.9	74.1
Philippines (1960–1980)	−30.8	130.8
South Korea (1963–1980)	65.7	34.3
Taiwan (1960–1980)	74.9	25.1

SOURCES: See sources of Table 7.5.

The rate of labor inflow into the services sector is rather high, even in South Korea and Taiwan. It should be kept in mind, however, that the services sector includes both the "formal services sector" such as finance and insurance which is induced by industrial activity and the "informal services sector" which functions as the sole absorber of the surplus labor force. The rate of labor inflow into the former is high in the case of South Korea and Taiwan, while the rate of labor inflow into the latter is high for Indonesia and the Philippines.

The concept of the informal services sector cannot be applied to existing statistics. We must therefore make a somewhat daring assumption that the labor force of the formal services sector includes labor in the commercial sector (L_{SC}) and the transportation, telecommunications, and financial sectors (L_{ST}), while the labor force in the informal service sector includes labor in the remaining individual services sectors (L_{SI}). The commercial sector and the transportation, telecommunications, and financial sectors have relatively strong linkages with the economic activities of modern sectors such as the manufacturing industries. In other words, L_{SC} and L_{ST} are the services sectors which flourish in response to an increase in the modern sectors' "derived demand for labor." On the other hand, the individual services sector is an important sector in that it has a huge reserve of low-wage labor and, therefore, has a notable tendency to dwindle as the economy grows. It is for this reason that the former is classified as the formal services sector while the latter is classified as the informal services sector. Based on this assumption, Table 7.7 shows the labor force in each respective sector as a share of the total labor force in all services sectors (L_S). There is a marked contrast between the two groups of countries, South Korea–Taiwan and the Philippines–Indonesia. The share of the individual services sector (L_{SI}/L_S) in the former group of countries is 2–21 percent whereas for the latter group it is as high as 69–86 percent.

It may be concluded from these observations that, in the case of the Asian

Table 7.7
Shares in the Services Sector of the Workers Out-Migrated
from the Agricultural Sector in Selected Asian Countries (percentage)

	L_{SC}/L_S	L_{ST}/L_S	L_{SI}/L_S
Indonesia (1971–1980)	—————30.7—————		69.3
Philippines (1960–1980)	11.2	2.7	86.1
South Korea (1963–1980)	52.8	26.2	21.0
Taiwan (1960–1980)	78.4	19.7	1.9

SOURCES: See sources of Table 7.5.

NIEs, the industrial sector has created numerous employment opportunities and has absorbed the labor force migrating out of the agricultural sector. On the other hand, the industrial sector in the Southeast Asian countries has offered less employment opportunities, and industrial wages have been kept at a lower level. However, more and more workers leave the agricultural sector and become concentrated mainly in the services sector and, to a lesser degree, in other nonagricultural sectors. As shown in Figure 7.1, where the real wage index of the industrial sector is compared with the cumulative index of the labor outflow from the agricultural sector, an increase in the cumulative index of the labor outflow from agriculture apparently coincides with an increase in the industrial wage rate in South Korea and Taiwan. In the Philippines and Thailand, however, the migration of the agricultural labor force has continued to increase despite a stagnant or declining wage rate in the industrial sector.

Urban Informal Sector and Slums

The agricultural labor force moves toward cities, particularly to the metropolitan area. In the case of the Philippines, a typical example of the metropolitan area is Metro Manila. Metro Manila is the economic center of the country where most of the economic activities are highly concentrated. It is natural for the agricultural labor force to come to Metro Manila and seek "crumbs of bread" that fall out of the economic activities in the metropolitan area. Of all the cities in the Philippines, Metro Manila has exhibited the strongest absorptive power in pulling population out of the rural areas.

In the case of Indonesia, the corresponding metropolitan area is Jakarta. People leaving various regions of Indonesia have tended to choose Jakarta as the place to move to (Table 7.8). Jakarta has become an extremely important city of in-migration not only for the people in Java Island but also for those in the outer islands of Sumatra, Kalimantan, and Sulawesi. The majority of these in-migrant workers are absorbed into the urban informal sector, which

Figure 7.1 REAL WAGE INDEX IN THE INDUSTRIAL SECTOR AND THE OUTFLOW OF AGRICULTURAL LABOR FORCE IN ASIA

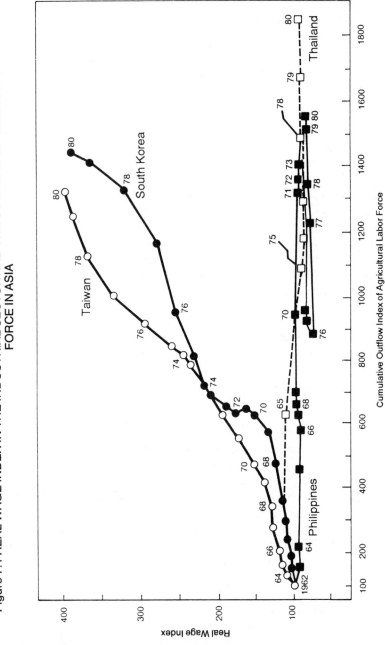

SOURCE :   See sources of Table 7.5.

Table 7.8
Areas of Largest Net In-Migration by Place
of Birth, Indonesia

PLACE OF BIRTH	AREA OF LARGEST IN-MIGRATION
Aceh	Jakarta
North Sumatra	Jakarta
West Sumatra	Jakarta
Riau	Jakarta
Jambi	Jakarta
South Sumatra	Lampung
Bengkulu	Jakarta
Lampung	Jakarta
Jakarta	Lampung
West Java	Jakarta
Central Java	Jakarta
Jogjakarta	Lampung
East Java	Lampung
Bali	Lampung
West Nusa Tenggara	Jakarta
East Nusa Tenggara	Jakarta
West Kalimantan	Jakarta
Central Kalimantan	Jakarta
South Kalimantan	Central Kalimantan
East Kalimantan	Jakarta
North Sulawesi	Jakarta
Central Sulawesi	Jakarta
South Sulawesi	Jambi
Southeast Sulawesi	Maluku
Maluku	Jakarta
Irian Jaya	Jakarta

SOURCE: Sundrum, R. M. 1976. Inter-Provincial Migration. *Bulletin of Indonesian Economic Studies* 12(1).

consists of street vendors, repairmen, and day laborers. For most workers, providing these services are an essential source of their livelihood whether it is carried out individually or by a family. Since the formal sector, which is led by the manufacturing industry, does not have a sufficient absorptive capacity of labor, the migrant workers from the rural area cannot find employment anywhere else but in the informal sector, the main characteristic of which is ease of entry. In fact, it can be said that this sector is being expanded by new migrant workers who squeeze themselves into the given volume of total employment. In this sense, the informal sector functions as a "safety valve" against consequences of growing overurbanization.

A 1976 survey conducted by the University of the Philippines on the informal services sector in Metro Manila revealed that 61 percent of the workers in this sector were migrants from outside Metro Manila. Similarly, in the case of Indonesia, those coming to Jakarta from the rural area were mostly employed in the informal sector. Table 7.9 shows the various occupations in Jakarta in which the majority of migrant workers from each of 14 villages in West Java are engaged in. The informal sector is apparently the leading sector. Overurbanization in Jakarta is, in reality, characterized by the swelling informal sector due to a large influx of population from the rural area.

The movement of people toward Jakarta was not caused by an abundant pool of attractive employment opportunities in the city, but rather was due to the lack of employment opportunities in the rural area which acted to "push" people out to the city. According to a survey conducted by the Socio-Economic Institute of Indonesia (LEKNAS–LIPI) on migrants in Jakarta, the majority of migrant workers cited "the lack of employment opportunities" as the most important reason for out-migration from the rural area (for example, 68 percent of beca (tricycle) drivers and 41 percent of peddlers). Urbanization in Java is characterized by a push-type of urbanization whereby the poverty and the lack of employment opportunities in the rural area push agricultural workers out to the city rather than a pull-type of urbanization where the city provides numerous opportunities for employment and thereby absorbs agricultural workers from the rural area.

Table 7.9

Most Popular Occupations of Migrants into Jakarta: Fourteen Village Cases
by Origin of Migration (percentage)

VILLAGE	SAMPLE MIGRANTS	OCCUPATION IN JAKARTA	PROPORTION IN SAMPLE MIGRANTS
I	74	Peanuts seller	65
II	55	Food and cigarette seller	35
III	91	Food seller	43
IV	70	Beca (tricycle) driver	57
V	82	Beca (tricycle) driver	41
VI	100	Day laborer	35
VII	87	Kerosene seller	32
VIII	77	Aircraft and hotel worker	32
IX	87	Grocer	60
X	88	Driver	27
XI	87	Beca (tricycle) driver	38
XII	92	Carpenter	49
XIII	99	Barber	31
XIV	104	Bread seller	42

SOURCE: Hugo, G. 1977. Circular Migration. *Bulletin of Indonesian Economic Studies* 8(3).

Poverty in the informal sector is symbolized by slums. One of the biggest slums in Southeast Asia is Tondo which spreads along the seashore in North Manila. It is an area with stench and noise, and countless number of huts made of used materials (these huts are called *barong-barong* in Tagalog) stand side-by-side with no space between them. Back in the 1950s, Tondo is said to have been a beautiful seaside area with thick coconut trees and only about ten houses. However, a large number of migrants from the provinces started pouring into the area in the 1960s. Today, Tondo has become a slum of 15,000 people. Because the slum population has been increasing recently at an annual rate of 12 percent, the ratio of the slum population to the total city population is on the continuous increase and there are a large number of big slum areas other than Tondo in Metro Manila (Figure 7.2). People living in slums now constitute 35 percent of the total population of Metro Manila.

There are also a large number of slums scattered over Metro-Bangkok. Khlong-Toey Slum is the biggest with about 40,000 residents who are living over the marshlands in the port of Khlong-Toey facing the Gulf of Thailand. Barracks made with wood and sheet zinc have been erected, and passageways are constructed by laying panel boards. Slum residents in Tondo or Khlong-Toey are called squatters, persons who illegally occupy public land. The squatters live unstable lives because they are constantly faced with the possibility of an eviction order.

Even more tragic situations can be found in Asia, particularly in the slum areas of the South Asian countries such as India and Bangladesh. In Dacca, the capital city of Bangladesh, more than 20 percent of the population live in slums and most of the slum residents are migrants from the rural area. Slum areas are located mainly on illegally occupied land, and is largely concentrated among public facilities such as railways, roads, train stations, and stadiums (Figure 7.3). Life in the slums is wretched. Public facilities such as roads, electricity, water, drainage, and disinfection services are not being provided to the residents. Schools and clinics are never constructed.

According to a survey conducted by the University of Dacca, 96 percent of the families living in slums in Dacca do not have kerosene lamps and 98 percent do not even have toilets. The survey also revealed that 74 percent of the families do not own any furniture, and only 5 percent and 4 percent have radios and clocks, respectively. The work of these people cannot possibly be called an "occupation." Since the number of work opportunities is insufficient, people rush like ants swarming to sweets to any available work they can find as a street vendor, peddler, barber, repairman, ragman, maid, rikshawman, and day laborer.

The greater part of Bangladesh is composed of the alluvial delta formed by three big rivers, namely, the Ganges, Brahmaputra, and Meghna. Because of these rivers, the ground is rather soft and it is difficult to con-

Figure 7.2 SLUMS IN MANILA METROPOLITAN AREA, PHILIPPINES

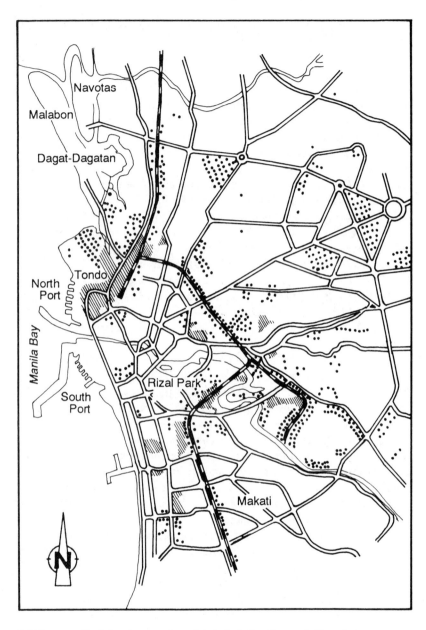

NOTE :   Shaded portions are slums. Dots indicate illegally occupied (squatter) areas.

SOURCE :   Nippon Hoso Shuppan Kyokai. 1984. *21-Seiki wa Keikoku Suru* [*Warnings from the 21st century*]. Tokyo: Nippon Hoso Shuppan Kyokai.

Figure 7.3 SLUMS IN DACCA, BANGLADESH

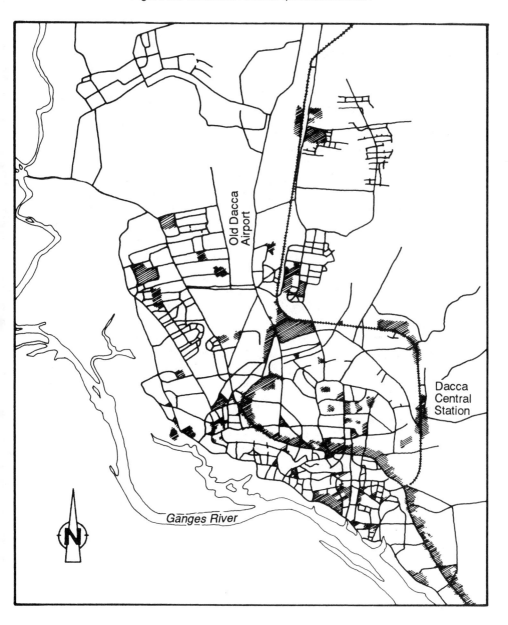

NOTE :   Shaded portions indicate slums.

SOURCE :   Qadir, S. R. 1975. *Bastees of Dacca: A Study of Squatter Settlement*. Dacca: Local
             Government Institute.

struct a road that is able to support the weight of automobiles. Thus, stones or similarly hard materials are very valuable. Cracked bricks are typically spread over roads so that they are able to support the weight of automobiles. People who crack the bricks into pieces are called brick-crackers and are employed by intermediary agents who are subcontracted by public enterprises for road construction. Brick-cracking, which can be done by women and children, is the lowest form of manual labor and is engaged in only when no other job alternatives can be found. Remuneration for brick-cracking is extremely low and almost the same as the "income" of a beggar. One is often asked for small change by grimy hands with many calluses when one passes by a construction site. There is only a very slight difference between a brick-cracker and a beggar, and both are faced with the harsh realities of life. Even if these people become weary of life in the slums, they have nowhere else to go. According to a published report, 62 percent of the slum residents expect their lives to remain the same and see no prospect of an improved standard of living.

This situation cannot be helped. These people did not come to Dacca because they were attracted by the job opportunities and wages, but because they had no prospect of employment at home due to extreme poverty in the rural area. Thus, they had no other alternative but to come to Dacca and settle down with no decent prospects in sight. The absolute lack of job opportunities in the rural area actually "pushed" the rural population to the city. Therefore, poverty in the city should be understood in the same context as poverty in the rural area. Poverty in the city is at the receiving end of poverty from the rural area.

It can be concluded that the expansion of the urban informal sector reflects the weak labor absorptive capacity of the urban formal sector as represented by the industrial sector. The previous chapter looked at the reasons why industrialization in Asian countries has a weak labor absorptive capacity. In looking at the predicament of the urban poor in this chapter, it seems that Asian countries urgently need a development strategy which will maximize their labor absorptive capacity.

CHAPTER EIGHT

Challenges by the Nies

From *"Choon Goong"* (Spring Poverty) to "Catch Up"

South Korea, which has been referred to a number of times in previous chapters, acquired its current economic power over the last twenty-odd years since the 1960s. At the beginning of this period, South Korea was in a state of extreme poverty. It was an underdeveloped country with scarce natural resources and a surplus population and labor force. It was also deprived of the basic conditions for modern economic growth partly because it had been under oppressive colonial rule. Today, its economic power is so strong that it often causes severe economic friction with developed countries. The economic development of this country has shown that even a country handicapped by adverse initial conditions and limited natural resources can achieve great success once its economy is skillfully managed. Thus South Korea's development process can provide many insights into the alternative patterns of future development of other developing countries in Asia, and the experience of South Korea is a valuable one for other countries in the contemporary developing world.

The whole area of the Korean Peninsula had been under Japanese colonial rule for 36 years since it was annexed by Japan in 1910. The phrase "36 years of Japanese Imperialism" still lingers in the hearts of South Koreans. Japanese control over the Korean Peninsula during the 36 years was indeed oppressive. For example, the Korean Company Ordinance, which was proclaimed in 1911 immediately after the Japanese annexation, had as its purpose the "suppression of indigenous industries." The Ordinance prescribed that no company in Korea could be established without a sanction from the Office of the Government-General in Korea, which was the center of Japanese colonial rule. With this Ordinance, the Office retained the legal right to suspend and prohibit business activities of Korean companies and to dissolve companies. Japan's intent was to make the colonized Korean Peninsula a base for supplying Japan with food and industrial materials and a market for industrial goods exported from Japan.

However, this policy of industrial suppression was gradually relaxed and, in 1920, the Korean Company Ordinance was abolished. Japanese entrepreneurs who had accumulated capital resources during World War I (1914–

1918) began to establish their production bases in colonized Korea. Thus progress was made in the industrialization of the colony in the 1920s. After the Manchurian incident in 1931 and the Sino-Japanese War in 1937, Japanese entrepreneurs extended their business activities on a large scale to Manchuria and China. This time Japan aimed at transforming colonized Korea into a logistic base and made further progress in its industrialization. Nevertheless, it was still the industrialization of a Japan-controlled colony. In fact, although Korean companies constituted 41 percent of all companies in the Peninsula in terms of number, their share in terms of paid-in capital and production was only 9 percent and 17 percent, respectively. Ownership of capital was almost totally monopolized by the Japanese.

Japanese monopoly, however, was not limited to capital ownership alone. The Japanese also monopolized positions of middle management and engineers let alone those of top management. Korean workers were engaged only in low-class manual labor. They had extremely limited opportunities for acquiring skills and enhancing their ability in business management. Consequently, the shortage of entrepreneurs, managers, and engineers became a severe constraint for the economic development of South Korea after its independence. The Japanese educational policy implemented in colonized Korea was a kind of "obscurantist policy" and had no intention of promoting secondary and higher education. *Samil Undong* (3–1 Movement), which began on March 1, 1919, was the first nationwide resistance movement against Japanese rule over Korea. In the wake of this violent resistance, Japan's colonial rule in Korea gradually shifted from an obscurantist policy to a "cultural policy." Under this cultural policy, the One-Village One-Elementary School Establishment Program was implemented. However, when the program was completed in 1936, the enrollment ratio of children in elementary schools in Korea was only 25 percent. The final outcome of the cultural policy as a whole was no better than this level.

After 36 years of colonial rule, Korea was liberated in 1945. However, the exuberance of the Korean people was short-lived with the outbreak of the Korean War in 1950. The Korean War was a typical war fought on the strength of material superiority, where all modern heavy weapons, with the exception of nuclear weapons, were used. The war brought about devastating damage that was unprecedented in modern warfare. The scale of physical destruction during the Korean War was estimated to equal two years of South Korea's gross domestic product at that time. However, more important may be the fact that a north-south division of Korea was formalized by this war. As pointed out earlier, there was some advance in industrialization in Korea even under Japanese colonial rule, but the advance in industrialization was mainly confined to northern Korea. Major underground resources were also concentrated in the north. Southern Korea at that time had only agriculture and a few light industries. "Industrial north and agricultural south" describes the structural characteristics of the Korean Peninsula following the war.

Due to the north-south division of Korea after the war, South Korea was no longer able to have a share of the assets left by the colonial rule. Thus, South Korea was totally deprived of the basic conditions necessary for modern economic growth that had been slowly building during the 36 years of colonial rule and the subsequent Korean War. South Korea had to start its economic growth virtually from nothing. Poverty was severe with the surplus population, and per capita income was even below the average level of Asian countries at that time. There were a large number of farmers suffering from *choon goong* (spring poverty). These farmers were often on the verge of starvation since they typically ate all of their foodstuffs before the spring harvest. It was beyond one's imagination then that South Korea would achieve its current level of high economic growth.

South Korea, having internationally well-known big businesses like Samsung, Hyundai, and Daewoo, is now economically catching up with developed countries. In 1985, passenger cars produced by Hyundai Automobile took the largest share for foreign car markets in Canada and Australia by surpassing Japanese cars. In 1986, Hyundai automobiles landed in the United States and achieved a big sales record. These achievements finally culminated in the Seoul Olympics in 1988. It is being said that South Korea plans to obtain the status of a developed country both in name and reality by joining the OECD (Organisation for Economic Co-operation and Development). What then was the process by which South Korea became what it is today?

Export-Oriented Industrialization

Two essential terms in discussing the economic development of South Korea are "export-oriented industrialization" and "heavy and chemical industrialization." South Korea started its first Five-Year Economic Development Plan in 1962 following a military coup d'etat. Since then, it has continuously adopted an export-oriented industrialization policy, a strategy to achieve growth through an active expansion of exports of industrial goods. In truth, South Korea did not have any alternative for economic development. After the north-south division, the country inherited only a poor rural area with a surplus population. In order to develop the economy under these circumstances, it was necessary to import a large amount of materials such as machinery and equipment, and exports were required to pay for these imports. Furthermore, since South Korea's domestic market was extremely limited because of the people's low income level, exports were indispensable. Export expansion was, so to speak, South Korea's "lifeline" for economic development.

Fortunately for South Korea, the world economy was at the height of simultaneous expansion in the 1960s when South Korea started its export-oriented industrialization. The United States, Japan, and the EC were all experiencing continued vigorous expansion, an expansion that had rarely been seen during the previous two hundred years of the capitalist world. These developed countries also had turbulent changes in their industrial structures. Newly growing industries emerged one after another while a number of other industries declined. The majority of declining industries in developed countries were labor-intensive industries and these suffered from an upward trend in wages. South Korea was fully convinced that it would be able to export labor-intensive products on a large scale towards the markets of developed countries. In addition to the decline of labor-intensive industries in developed countries, the market for labor-intensive goods was further stimulated by increased demand arising from the high economic growth of the developed countries. South Korea indeed showed its excellent skills in projecting a new international market environment and in being able to actively pursue a policy of export-oriented industrialization in response to a favorable market environment.

The South Korean strategy is in clear contrast with the policy attitude that was common in other developing countries at that time. After World War II, most developing countries adopted a protectionist policy called import-substituting industrialization which was discussed in Chapter 6. In these countries, the plan was to foster domestic industries which produce goods for domestic markets that were heavily protected by their governments. This protectionist pattern of industrialization was partly due to a kind of export pessimism. International markets for industrial products were totally dominated by developed countries at that time, and it was totally unthinkable for developing countries to increase their exports and compete effectively with the industries of developed countries. Almost all developing countries which aimed at industrialization restricted imports from developed countries and thereby kept their domestic markets exclusively for domestic industries, to which governments offered various protective measures.

However, under the government's heavy protection, these industries failed to make any effort to increase production efficiency. A small domestic market, which was deliberately created by protection, immediately became saturated. Thus, industrialization in these developing countries fell into serious stagnation soon after it was launched. Nevertheless, most developing countries did not readily change their policies. Although a favorable international market existed during the 1960s, only a few countries, which are currently called the Asian NIEs, succeeded in finding a path of development through export expansion. South Korea is a typical example.

As shown in Figure 8.1, exports of South Korea have increased at an extremely rapid pace over the past twenty years. Not only has the absolute value of exports risen dramatically, but the share of exports in the national economy has also greatly increased. South Korea's degree of dependence upon exports—namely, the ratio of exports to gross domestic product—rose from merely a few percent in the early 1960s to 40 percent in recent years.

Although the industrial base in South Korea was initially immature and fragile, the country actively tried to expand its export of industrial goods. It follows that South Korea had to resort to a processing trade. In a processing trade, materials and intermediate goods that are imported from developed countries are assembled or processed using machinery and equipment which are also imported from developed countries; then the final products are exported. South Korea's industrial structure has inevitably become that of a processing trade. Under such an industrial structure, export expansion simultaneously induced a large increase in imports. Figure 8.1 shows that, in spite of a considerable increase in exports, South Korea had a trade deficit until 1986 because of its larger volume of imports.

Japan, which neighbors South Korea and produces a large amount of parts, semimanufactured goods, machinery, and equipment, has been the most important source of supply for South Korea's demand for imports. South Korea would not have been able to pursue economic development through a processing trade without industrial goods imported from Japan (Table 8.1). Although South Korea's total net exports (exports less imports) of industrial goods has been in large surplus since 1975, its net exports of industrial goods to Japan has been in large deficit, particularly in capital goods like machinery and equipment. The deficit with Japan is also large in net exports of intermediate goods such as parts and semimanufactured products. On the other hand, South Korea has a large trade surplus with the world and particularly with the United States. Therefore, it can be said that South Korea has pursued economic development through a processing trade, whereby it imports parts, semimanufactured goods, machinery, and equipment from Japan, and exports consumers goods, which are assembled and processed from the imported Japanese materials, that are mainly destined for the United States. In other words, the imported Japanese parts, semimanufactured goods, machinery, and equipment have been "built into" South Korea's structure of a processing trade. In this regard, it would be correct to say that South Korea's economic development has been dependent upon various imports from Japan. However, this is not the issue to be emphasized here.

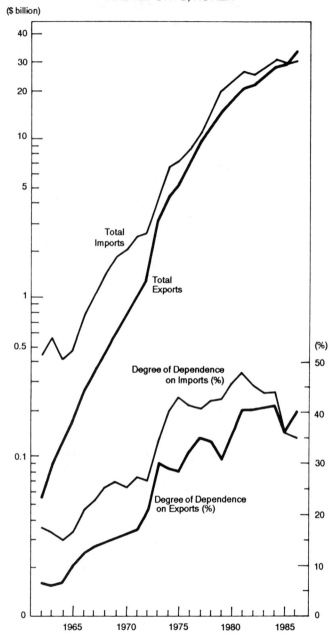

Figure 8.1 TOTAL EXPORTS AND IMPORTS AND THE DEGREE OF DEPENDENCE ON EXPORTS AND IMPORTS, KOREA

SOURCE :   Korea, Economic Planning Board. *Korea Statistical Yearbook.* Seoul: EPB.

Table 8.1

Net Exports (Exports–Imports) of Industrial Goods in South Korea
(US$ millions)

	1962	1965	1970	1975	1980	1984
Nondurable consumer goods						
World	1	33	328	1,576	4,376	6,418
Japan	1	1	42	222	514	829
United States	–	22	233	672	1,710	2,147
Durable consumer goods						
World	–18	–3	–88	214	1,524	2,486
Japan	–8	–3	–62	–112	–350	–614
United States	–6	–1	–1	203	748	1,221
Intermediate goods						
World	–159	–110	–247	–222	2,129	3,450
Japan	–60	–101	–291	–827	–1,161	–1,847
United States	–71	–21	20	196	281	563
Capital goods						
World	–56	–54	–453	–1,178	–2,201	–3,005
Japan	–28	–32	–242	–723	–1,867	–2,522
United States	–15	–7	–74	–283	–344	–811
Total						
World	–236	–134	–460	375	5,738	9,349
Japan	–98	–136	–553	–1,445	–3,172	–4,154
United States	–94	–5	177	782	2,372	3,120

NOTE: – indicates net imports.
SOURCE: United Nations. *Yearbook of International Trade Statistics.* New York: UN.

While Korea has been dependent on Japan, it is important to point out
that South Korea has actually gained strength in terms of economic self-reliance. The right-hand side of Figure 8.2 shows that the export-import ratio in
South Korea's trade of industrial goods with Japan was very low until only
about ten years ago. At that time, South Korea one-sidedly imported industrial goods from Japan, and almost none of South Korea's industrial products were exported to Japan. But this ratio has rapidly increased within a
short period of time, and today, the ratio for total industrial goods has
reached about 40 percent. Although South Korea's trade deficit with Japan
increased to US$5.4 billion in 1986, it is expected to decrease to US$1.5 billion in 1991 according to the plan by the Ministry of Trade and Industry of
South Korea. This plan appears to be feasible, and it is expected that the
export-import ratio in South Korea's trade with Japan will gradually reach
100 percent in the not-too-distant future.

Figure 8.2 EXPORT/IMPORT RATIO OF KOREA'S INDUSTRIAL GOODS

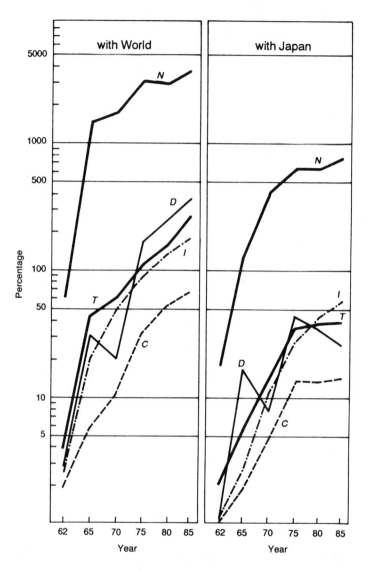

NOTES :   N : Nondurable consumer goods
          D : Durable consumer goods
          I : Intermediate goods
          C : Capital goods
          T : Total industrial goods

SOURCE :   United Nations. *Yearbook of International Trade Statistics.*
           New York: UN.

The upward trend of the export-import ratio in South Korea's trade of industrial goods with Japan indicates that the trade relationship between South Korea and Japan has been gradually changing from South Korea's one-sided dependency on Japan to that of mutual dependency. The change towards such a balanced trade of industrial goods between the two countries can be interpreted as a change in the economic relationship between South Korea and Japan from that of a vertical division of labor to a horizontal division of labor. It is clearly seen in this changing relationship that South Korea's economy is moving in the direction of economic self-reliance. Although South Korea initially pursued export-oriented industrialization with an overwhelming dependence upon Japanese parts, semimanufactured goods, machinery, and equipment, it is now producing these input materials and goods domestically and is even exporting them in large volume. As shown in the left-hand side of Figure 8.2, the export-import ratio in South Korea's trade of industrial goods with the world has already exceeded 100 percent for intermediate goods (not to mention consumers goods) and has reached as high as 60 percent for capital goods.

South Korea's move towards economic self-reliance can be seen in terms of introduction of foreign capital as well. As was shown in Figure 8.1, the trade balance of South Korea has been persistently in deficit. However, the South Korean government did not adopt a policy of import reduction to rectify the trade deficit. Had its imports been reduced, its economy might have eventually contracted since the imports are mainly composed of essential capital goods like machinery and equipment. Instead, South Korea adopted an active policy of introducing foreign capital to compensate for its trade deficit. Without such an expansionist approach to economic management, South Korea could not have achieved high economic growth. Thus, the degree of contribution of foreign capital to domestic investment in South Korea was extremely high (Figure 8.3). Such a high degree of dependence upon foreign capital was unprecedented in the history of any developed country. In fact, South Korea is known as a country of huge external debt, next to three Latin American countries, namely, Brazil, Mexico, and Argentina. This high level of debt indicates that South Korea introduced a very large amount of foreign capital in the past.

However, South Korea has been clearly reducing its dependence upon foreign capital. As shown in Figure 8.3, except for the two periods of the world oil crises in the mid-1970s and around 1980, the degree of South Korea's dependence upon foreign capital has been decreasing fairly rapidly while the rate of domestic investment has been increasing at an extremely high speed. Although South Korea still has a huge amount of external debt, the amount is now rapidly decreasing through its aggressive repayments since 1985.

South Korea was able to reduce its degree of dependence upon foreign

Figure 8.3 SHARE OF FOREIGN CAPITAL IN KOREA'S TOTAL INVESTMENT

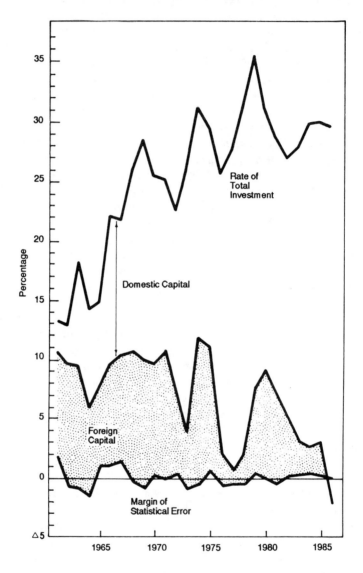

NOTE :   Δ indicates negative.

SOURCE :   Korea, Economic Planning Board. *Korea Statistical Yearbook.* Seoul: EPB.

capital through a gradual accumulation of domestic capital resources obtained under high economic growth. Figure 8.4 clearly shows that the ratio of domestic saving to total domestic investment has been gradually rising.

Heavy and Chemical Industrialization and Economic Self-Reliance

South Korea's move towards economic self-reliance is more vividly shown by its progress in heavy and chemical industrialization. A processing-trade type of economy should be regarded as a non-self-reliant economy since it depends on imports of essential industrial goods such as parts, semimanu-factured goods, machinery, and equipment.

An economy cannot be self-reliant unless it is able to produce the essential basic materials and goods within the country. In other words, as long as an economy depends upon a processing trade, the strength of its growth does not impact much on the domestic economy but mostly leaks out of the country. Since an increase in exports will strongly induce more imports of input materials under a processing trade structure, a better balance of trade cannot be expected. In addition, a widely open economy tends to become vulnerable to external instability since the whole economy fluctuates in response to changes in overseas market conditions. Therefore, efforts must be made to establish a production base for materials and intermediate and capital goods in order to build a self-reliant national economy. These objectives can be realized only through heavy and chemical industrialization.

In fact, there has been a remarkable advance in South Korea's heavy and chemical industrialization since the early 1970s. To see the speed of progress in heavy and chemical industrialization, we can use Hoffmann's ratio. The Hoffmann's ratio is defined as the ratio of total value added in light industry to total value added in the heavy and chemical industries. According to Professor Walter G. Hoffmann, it took 20–30 years for developed countries to move from the first phase of industrialization, as indicated by a Hoffmann's ratio between 5.0 and 3.5, to the second phase where the ratio falls between 3.5 and 1.5. However, it was only within a few years in the 1960s when this ratio for South Korea dropped from 4.0 to 2.0 (Figure 8.5). Then, around 1970, South Korea entered into the third phase of industrialization as indicated by a ratio between 1.5 and 0.5. Thus, South Korea moved from the second to the third phase of industrialization within only a few years, and the speed of the transition was three to four times faster than that experienced by developed countries. Thus, South Korea's industrialization can be considered to be a compressed pattern of industrial development.

Large-scale heavy and chemical industrialization has been promoted in South Korea since the 1970s. In 1972, the third Five-Year Economic Devel-

Figure 8.4 GROSS INVESTMENT AND DOMESTIC SAVING RATES, KOREA

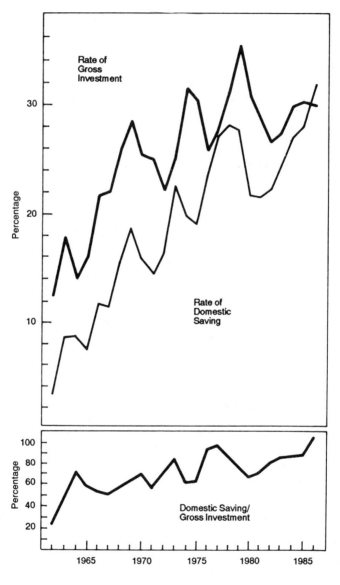

SOURCE :   Korea, Economic Planning Board. *Korea Statistical Yearbook.* Seoul: EPB.

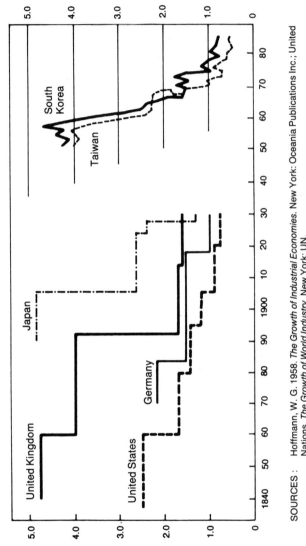

Figure 8.5 INTERNATIONAL COMPARISON OF HOFFMANN'S RATIOS

SOURCES :   Hoffmann, W. G. 1958. *The Growth of Industrial Economies.* New York: Oceania Publications Inc.; United Nations. *The Growth of World Industry.* New York: UN.

opment Plan was started. The main feature of this plan was the strong emphasis on heavy and chemical industrialization. In 1973, the South Korean government announced that it would embark on a program of large-scale heavy and chemical industrialization, and the government designated the steel, nonferrous metals, oil, machinery, shipbuilding, and electronics industries as the six strategic industries. The heavy and chemical industrialization of South Korea was symbolized then by the Pohang Integrated Steel Mill whose first phase of construction work was completed in July 1973. The size of this steel mill expanded considerably with the completion of the second phase in 1976 and the third phase in 1978. Today, it has become one of the largest and the most modern integrated steel mills in the world. South Korea still has a big domestic demand for steel and its production capacity for steel increased further with the completion of the Second Pohang Integrated Steel Mill in 1987.

The speed of development of the steel industry of the advanced countries with that of latecomer countries is compared in Figure 8.6. The United Kingdom and Germany, which both started their steel industry around 1880 with an annual production capacity of a million tons of crude steel, needed 60 and 54 years, respectively, to achieve a production capacity of 15 million tons. It took 60 years for France to achieve the same capacity. Even the United States and Japan needed 24 and 34 years, respectively, although their steel industries had the most rapid expansion among developed countries. In contrast, it is anticipated that South Korea will need only a little more than ten years to achieve such a large-scale production capacity.

One of the factors for the rapid expansion of South Korea's heavy and chemical industrialization was its government policy of protection for heavy and chemical industries. The industries, which were designated by the Priority Industries Promotion Act as strategic development sectors, were given highly favorable tax and financial incentives which thereby enabled them to expand their production rapidly. However, we cannot help but refer to the international political environment surrounding South Korea, which was perhaps the most important factor for the rapid growth of South Korea's heavy and chemical industrialization. Its severe political rivalry with North Korea acted as a centripetal force for promoting national aspirations for a strong nation, and for promoting heavy and chemical industrialization which would support such a strong nation. In addition, the people and the military of South Korea became strongly aware of the urgent need for both economic and military self-reliance with the weakening of the United States' military commitment in the Korean Peninsula which accelerated in the 1970s when the phase-out plan of the U.S. forces stationed in South Korea was officially announced.

The withdrawal plan of the U.S. ground forces stationed in South Korea,

Figure 8.6 SPEED OF EXPANSION IN CAPACITY FOR STEEL PRODUCTION

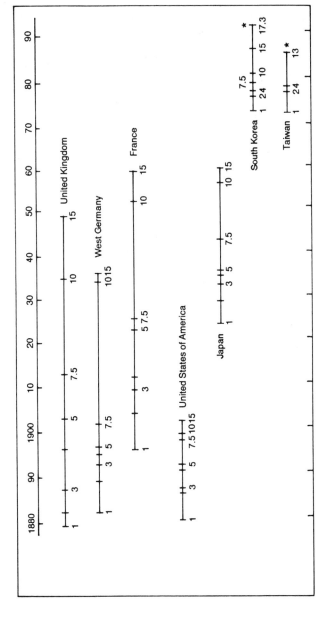

NOTE :   1,3,5, . . , 15 indicate 1,3,5, . . ., 15 million tons, respectively, in terms of crude steel production capacity.
         *indicates planned figures.

SOURCE :   Mitchell, B. R. 1982. *International Historical Statistics*. London: Macmillan Press.

which was announced simultaneously with the inauguration of the Carter Administration in January 1977, was the biggest political threat to South Korea after the Korean War. It was not by pure coincidence that South Korea's plan of heavy and chemical industrialization was carried out rapidly during this period. Thus, it can be said that strong aspirations for economic self-reliance and a formidable political and military environment surrounding South Korea were the major factors behind the promotion and rapid pace of South Korea's heavy and chemical industrialization.

CHAPTER NINE

Promoters of Miracle Growth

Propellants for Economic Progress in Newly Industrialized Economies

The previous chapter discussed economic progress in South Korea over the past two decades during which the principal promoters of growth were business conglomerates. Many of the South Korean conglomerates were established after Japanese rule over the Korean peninsula had come to an end in 1945. Despite their short histories, these conglomerates have rapidly expanded their business frontiers to the extent that they are now the dominant economic power in South Korea. It was indeed these conglomerates who played a most important role in pursuing the export-oriented and heavy and chemical industrialization which characterized the strategic thrust in economic development in South Korea. The South Korean conglomerates are now gaining enough strength to play a significant role in the domestic economy, and they are also internationally well-known as big businesses with increasing capacity to compete with multinational corporations from the industrialized countries.

South Korea is not the only country where business conglomerates are playing a prominent role in economic development. In many Asian countries, conglomerate-affiliated enterprises are currently playing an active role in their economies. This is particularly true in Southeast Asian countries where economic development cannot be discussed without mentioning the increasing presence of the overseas Chinese-related conglomerates. A list of the most powerful conglomerates in the East and Southeast Asian countries is given in Table 9.1. Although there are several indigenous conglomerates such as the Siam Cement Group in Thailand, the Ayala and Soriano Groups in the Philippines, and the Bakrie Group in Indonesia, the majority of the conglomerates in East and Southeast Asia are Chinese-related. These conglomerates are running gigantic business activities, and they are, in general, operated under family-related management. They are characterized by their premodern style of management including kinship personnel management, and majority shareholdings by their family and relatives who are literally called "tycoons" (feudal commander-in-chief).

It is inevitable that when a traditional society, where modern institutions are lacking, takes part in rapid industrialization, management systems have to be organized based upon the most fundamental social unit, i.e., family

Table 9.1
Major Industrial Conglomerates in East and Southeast Asia

COUNTRY/REGION	NAME OF CONGLOMERATE	NAME OF CORE ENTERPRISE (INDUSTRY)
Hong Kong	Li Jiacheng (C)	Cheng Jiang Enterprise (estates)
	Y. K. Pao (C)	Worldwide (shipping)
	C. H. Tong (C)	OOHL (shipping)
Taiwan	Taisu (C)	Taiwan Plastics (plastics)
	Da Tong (C)	Da Tong (electronics)
	Manfang-Tongyi (C)	Tainan Textile (textile)
	Yu Long (C)	Yu Long Motor (automobile)
Thailand	Bangkok Bank (C)	Bangkok Bank (bank)
	Siam Cement (L)	Siam Cement (cement)
	Siam Motor (C)	Siam Motor (automobile)
	Ransam (C)	Thai Farmers Bank (bank)
	Saha (C)	SPI (goods)/Saha Union (textiles)
Indonesia	Lim (C)	BCA (bank)
	Astra (C)	Astra (merchandise/trade)
	Rodamas (C)	Rodamas (merchandise/trade)
	Bakrie (L)	Bakrie (merchandise/trade)
	Soedarpo (L)	Soedarpo (shipping/trade)
Philippines	Ayala (L)	Ayala (stocks/trade)
	Soriano (L)	Anscor (stocks/trade)
	Yu Chengco (C)	RCBC (bank)
	L. Tang (C)	Allied Banking (bank)
Malaysia	Sime Darby (L)	Sime Darby (stocks)
	Kuok (C)	Kuok (stocks)
	MPH (C)	MPH (stocks)
	UMW (C)	UMW (stocks)
Singapore	OCBC (C)	OCBC (bank)
	UOB (C)	UOB (bank)
	Khoo Teck Puat (C)	Goodwood Park (hotel)
	Hong Leong (C)	Hong Leong (investment)
	Jack Chia (C)	Jack Chia:MPH (medicines)

NOTES: C = overseas Chinese merchants
L = local enterprise

SOURCE: Inoue, Ryuichiro, ed. 1987. *Ajia no Zaibatsu to Kigyo* [*Industrial corporations and companies in Asia*]. Nippon Keizai Shimbun-Sha: Tokyo.

members and relatives. Taking the South Korean conglomerates as an illustration, this chapter will discuss the principal propellants for industrialization in Asian countries.

According to the worldwide ranking (in terms of sales revenue) of large manufacturers which is published annually by *Fortune,* three Korean manufacturers—namely, Samsung (20th), Lucky/Gold-Star (32nd), and Daewoo (35th)—appeared in 1987 among the top fifty firms (excluding those firms from the United States). Likewise, thirteen Japanese manufacturers were found in the same list. The ranking indicates that some South Korean conglomerates have already acquired a gigantic scale of business that is comparable to typical multinational corporations. How did these conglomerates establish such powerful positions within such a short period of time? In the Korean peninsula where the Confucius culture was predominant, there was a tendency for people not to appreciate entrepreneurship in such a traditional value system. Furthermore, the rise of indigenous enterprises had been severely hampered under colonial rule. After the liberalization, the severe shortage of organized enterprises and the lack of manpower for undertaking enterprises were immediately evident. Nevertheless, enormous business opportunities were created during a period of reconstruction after the Korean War, followed by further opportunities during the high economic growth period which began in the early 1960s. Consequently, a vast amount of fertile land had to be cultivated by the self-efforts of a few individuals who possessed disciplined business minds and entrepreneurship capabilities. There were no tailor-made organizations to absorb the opportunities in the economy. Individual entrepreneurship was the only weapon to fight against unknown business frontiers.

Venture Capitalism

Many readers may know Mr. Chung Choo-Young, whose career is one of the most popular success stories in South Korean business circles. He is the absolute leader of the Hyundai conglomerate, and is the honorable Chairman of the Hyundai Group which has been playing a leading role in the process of heavy and chemical industrialization in South Korea. Both Mr. Chung's personal career as an entrepreneur and his current status in the business world could be seen as a symbolic miniature example that reflects the modern experiences of the South Korean economy.

Mr. Chung was born in Kangwon-do province in 1915 and had no formal education beyond elementary school. When he was 16 years old, he moved out of his village and worked in railway construction as an unskilled laborer, spending the whole day pulling a rear-car full of gravel. After working as a clerk in a rice milling–cum–retail shop, he started a rice merchandise business which, however, soon went bankrupt. Next, he became a general contractor for civil works with his own funds saved through pathetic endeavors. In 1950 he purchased a garage. Based on these two small businesses, he embarked on the management of the Hyundai Construction Company.

The first big chance for Mr. Chung's business was brought by the Korean War which started in 1950. The war presented numerous business opportunities for the Hyundai Construction Company that allowed the firm to grow from a small and frail company to a medium-sized firm. During the war,

Pusan, where the Hyundai Company was located, was a logistics base for the United Nations Army. This brought a lot of construction work for various facilities, and the Hyundai Construction Company was fortunate to be awarded several contracts for these civil works. Even after the Korean War, the demand for reconstruction work kept the Hyundai Company busy and brought about a rapid expansion in its business activities. It was the reconstruction work on the Han River bridge in 1957 which enabled the Hyundai Construction Company to catch up with other medium-sized general contractors, and the company was recognized for the first time as one of the best general contractors in South Korea. With the capital and technologies accumulated through this contract, the company became a leading firm in the construction industry in Korea. Finally the Hyundai Company gained the highest status in the construction industry when it was awarded a general contract for the construction of the Soyang river multipurpose dam project which was then considered to be the most difficult civil works project in the history of the construction industry in South Korea.

This rapid expansion was not confined to the domestic market. Since the latter half of the 1960s, the Hyundai Company gradually expanded its business frontiers overseas. The largest opportunity came when a contract was awarded in 1976 for the construction of Jubel industrial port in Saudi Arabia. This contract, which was believed to be the largest one in the world in the 20th century, was planned by the oil-rich government of Saudi Arabia. This was an epoch-making event in the sense that an unknown Korean firm broke into the international construction market in the Middle East where the "big five" general contractors had been dominating for a long time. Owing to the above, the Hyundai Construction Company became well-known throughout the world and has been called "Hyundai" ever since.

Together with the expansion of the Hyundai Construction Company, Mr. Chung also extended his business frontiers into various activities in the heavy and chemical industries. Mr. Chung established the Hyundai Car Manufacturing Company in 1967. This was followed by the construction of an integrated shipping yard in Ulsan in 1970 with a capacity of one million tons making it one of the largest yards in the world in those days. In 1975 the Hyundai Car Manufacturing Company successfully started domestic production of small passenger vehicles which were soon exported to Canada. In Canada and Australia, the number of imported cars from Korea soon surpassed those from Japan. As mentioned in the previous chapter, new model vehicles were first exported to the United States in 1988. Furthermore, the Hyundai Motor Company has diversified its investment to the extent that it plans to construct factories in the United States and Canada in 1988 and 1989, respectively. This expansion also illustrates another symbolic venture undertaken by the Hyundai Corporation towards the overseas market, paralleling the experience of the Jubel industrial port construction.

Having witnessed the progress of the Hyundai conglomerate, we should take note of the importance of Mr. Chung's keen insight in grasping business opportunities, and his aggressive entrepreneurship in translating these opportunities into business expansion. His talents were not only appreciated in those days when Hyundai was still a small-scale business, but continued to be appreciated when Hyundai became one of the largest enterprises in the world. The phenomenal success of the firm also rested with Mr. Chung's outstanding individual capability to overcome several potentially fatal crises for the company which occurred because of his excessively aggressive attitude towards new opportunities and his ambitious expansion plans. This individual trait is attributable not only to Mr. Chung but also to many other business tycoons including Mr. Lee Byung-Chul, founder of the Samsung Corporation who passed away in the autumn of 1987, and Mr. Kim Woo-Joong, head of the Daewoo Corporation.

One stage in the development of the South Korean conglomerates is portrayed by the venture stories in which a few talented entrepreneurs have untiringly explored vast business frontiers generated during the process of independence, the war, and the implementation of the government's economic plans. However, these conglomerates are no longer small-scale businesses in the infant stage of their development, and as such outstanding personalities must now play in accordance with the international standards of big business. In the following section, the management style the Korean conglomerates applied during their business expansion is discussed and analyzed.

Management Style of the South Korean Conglomerates

First, it should be pointed out that the Korean conglomerates are mostly managed by the founder's family and relatives who wholeheartedly adhere to their leader's individual insight and philosophy. The history of the South Korean conglomerates is short, and many of them are still managed by the founders themselves. Therefore, it may be possible to conclude that they are "young" in terms of institutional development, as they are still generally managed by the owner or the owner's family or relatives. At the same time, it should not be overlooked that the traditional kinship preference (nepotism), which is prevalent in countries like Korea where the Confucius value system is influential, is still strongly maintained in the management of firms. In any conglomerate, a closed-management system controlled by the owner's family and relatives is firmly established. In almost all affiliated enterprises, the position of president is occupied by the founder's children or relatives. There are very few cases where the presidency is executed by professional management staff who are not related to the founder by blood.

Nepotism or blood kinship in Japanese business society is not weak either.

However, in Japan, the motivation of sustaining family enterprises has been more important than the motivation of maintaining blood kinship, e.g., the exclusion of blood kinship occurred quite often in order to sustain family enterprises or assets. It was a usual practice among merchants in the Edo period (1603–1867) for the founder of family enterprises to be succeeded by adopted sons beyond the owner's blood relations. This traditional behavior has also been maintained in company management since the Meiji era (1868–1912), and there have been few cases in Japan where the owner's blood relatives took part directly in the management of corporations. Therefore in Japan, the transfer of managerial authority from the founder's family and relatives to the professional management staff was met with little resistance.

The corporate management by kinship in Korea, however, is ensured by the dominance of corporate shares by the founder's family. It is a primary feature of the Korean conglomerates that there is strong unity, rather than segregation, of management and ownership. Among the twenty-one major firms under the Hyundai conglomerate, four firms including the Hyundai Construction Company itself are dominated by Mr. Chung's family with his shareholdings amounting to more than 40 percent of total shares, while more than 20 percent of eleven firms' shares are held by his family (Table 9.2). The Hyundai Construction Company is the core of the conglomerate and is recognized as Mr. Chung's personal company (with his family's shareholdings being more than 47 percent). Because this company owns majority shares of many other firms under the conglomerate, it can be inferred that the majority shares of these firms are indirectly owned by Mr. Chung's family. Of the twenty-one firms, there are eleven firms with more than 40 percent of its shares held by Mr. Chung's family or the Hyundai Construction Company. For the remaining ten firms, there are many mutual shareholdings among the firms under the Hyundai conglomerate. This means that the number of shareholders who are not related to Mr. Chung by blood may be marginally small.

This is also true for the Samsung Conglomerate. It is said that Mr. Lee Byung-Chul and his family are controlling more than 40 percent of the aggregated shares of the affiliated firms registered under the Exchange Commission, while controlling more than 60 percent of the aggregate shares of unregistered affiliated firms. The control of shares by the founder's family means strong managerial control over the affiliated firms. Thus, majority shareholding is nothing but a means for managerial control.

The decision-making style of Korean corporations is, as a matter of course, a "top-down" procedure. This is especially true for matters relating to fundamental issues of the corporation—such as the establishment of a new company, the management of a new enterprise, partnership with foreign enterprises, and personnel action for senior staff of the affiliated firms—which

Table 9.2

Status of Shareholdings under the Hyundai Corporation, 1982

| | SHAREHOLDINGS BY | | |
NAME OF ENTERPRISE	MR. CHUNG (A)	HYUNDAI CO. (B)	TOTAL SHAREHOLDINGS (A+B)
Hyundai Construction	47	–	47
Hyundai Heavy Industry	27	3	30
Hyundai Motor	7	13	20
Hyundai Vehicles	4	2	6
Hyundai Electronics	4	8	12
Hyundai Engines	4	11	15
Hyundai Precision	17	43	60
Hyundai Motor Services	47	–	47
Hyundai Steel Pipe	6	70	76
Hyundai Cement	45	–	45
Hyundai Engineering	25	–	25
Hyundai Timber	3	70	73
Hyundai Trading	7	7	14
Haiia Construction	28	48	76
Korean Urban Development	34	52	86
Korean Pavement Construction	17	74	91
Inchon Steel Mill	1	9	10
Keuk-Dong Petroleum	25	–	25
Dong Suh Industry	28	27	55
Keum Kang Development	49	–	49
Hyundai Shipping	28	–	28

SOURCE: Hattori, Tamio, and Yasunori Omichi. 1985. *Kankoku no Kigyo: Hito to Keiei* [*Korean enterprises: personnel and management*]. Nippon Keizai Shimbun-Sha: Tokyo.

are, without exception, determined by the founder himself. The authority of subordinate management under the corporation is unbelievably limited compared with that of Japanese firms. The management merely act as "mediators" or "faithful executors" in response to the founders' decisions. This is in clear contrast with the Japanese style of the decision-making process in which formulation of a consensus within a firm is much respected by means of a "bottom-up" procedure: consensus formulated at the bottom is transmitted to the top decision makers for their consideration and approval.

At 5:30 A.M. everyday, Mr. Chung Choo-Young wakes up. At about six o'clock, two telephones installed in his bedroom start ringing one by one, bringing urgent messages from overseas branches as well as from executives on mission. It is Mr. Chung's order that the overseas branches and the executives on mission should discuss urgent and important matters with him over the phone between six and six-thirty in the morning. His direct instructions on overseas activities so early in the morning indicate his inborn diligence as well as his management style of quick response and decision-making regarding business activities. Ever since the formative period of the Hyundai Construction Company, Mr. Chung has believed in making quick decisions on the spot. There is no doubt that instant decision-making on the spot should be the most speedy and effective way of conducting business. Due to direct telephone conversations with Mr. Chung in the early morning, the overseas branches of the company can work as efficiently as if they were working in Seoul. It is said that these morning calls become more frequent on Sundays. Even day and night on Sundays, staff stationed at the headquarters receive telexes from the branches all over the world, and report them to Mr. Chung for his decision. (*Chosen Nippo Keizai Bu, Zaibastu 25 Ji* [*Korean conglomerates at 25 hours*]. 1985. Translated by Shinsuke Tsuru. Tokyo: Doyukan)

Although important matters relating to the management of conglomerates are "exclusively" decided by the founder himself, there is a limitation in terms of the owner taking part in every decision-making process of the expanded and complicated conglomerate to which many firms are affiliated. Therefore, the decision-making channels in Korean conglomerates have become institutionalized in recent years. Every conglomerate has now established a kind of central coordination unit which is variously called an executive meeting among the presidents, the chairman's secretariat, the group planning unit, and the comprehensive planning and coordination unit. The emergence of these coordination units, however, does not necessarily imply the delegation of decision-making authority to the lower level. On the contrary, this means nothing but the institutionalization of the top-down decision-making process intended by the founder adapted to the expanded and complicated systems under the conglomerates. These centrally controlled units are not provided with as much authority as it may appear, and they can function well only if they are supported by "the last resort," i.e., the founder's power and dignity.

The management style of the Korean conglomerates was highly adaptable to the process of rapid economic growth in the country. The South Korean economy has, so far, been in an era of quantitative expansion. The past behavior adopted by the Hyundai Construction Company was ideally suited to this expansion with big contracts being awarded for national projects in the infrastructure and heavy and chemical industry sectors, and promotion of construction exports, particularly to the Middle East. Without speedy and timely top-down decision making, it would have been impossible to grasp these business opportunities and to expand the sphere of the business domain. The slow but steady bottom-up procedure in decision making, which requires consensus at the bottom level, may not be suitable for a period of expansion. Of course, it may be said that a decision-making process solely concentrated upon the top-head may be risky, and in fact, there were a few conglomerates which made a promising debut but soon sank into the deep sea. For example, the Kukje Corporation which had been ranked 9th in terms of sales revenue in 1984, was dissolved after a serious financial crisis. The experiences of this firm demonstrate that the Korean economy itself did not undergo steady growth of business but experienced a stormy era of rising capitalism.

Today the South Korean economy has stepped into an era where it must explore its own means of promoting exports of highly sophisticated technology products such as automobiles and electronics. The scale of Korean exports has become so large in the international market that merchandise exports, on the basis of mass production with price competitiveness, face harsh import restrictions imposed by developed countries. At the same time, comparative advantages in standardized technologies and cheap labor are shifting to the ASEAN countries and China. Therefore, Korea is now being attacked by both sides; namely, protective markets in developed countries and the ever-increasing competition from the less developed countries. There is no doubt that the Korean economy has progressed into a phase where it has to export higher value-added and quality products, particularly automobiles, electronics, and machinery.

A decisive factor for increasing competitiveness among technologically sophisticated products would be the adoption of quality and processing control which could only be achieved at the workshop level of the manufacturing process. The information and technology improvement required for this may not fit with the traditional style of top-down management. Therefore the most important task for the Korean conglomerates would be to adopt a more systematic and fine-tuned management style at the production level; this would include an improvement in cohesion among staff at all production levels including technicians and foremen, and the promotion of professional staff's participation in managerial decision making by means of delegation of authority.

The South Korean economy is in a transition from a quantitatively expanding period to a "qualitatively deepening phase." This implies that Korea is experiencing a change from an era of scale economies to an era of better management. How will the conglomerates respond to this challenge? This is a major question that is faced not only by Korea but also by the Southeast Asian countries. The future of the conglomerates may depend on the answer to this question.

CHAPTER TEN

Revived Household Farming

New Agriculture Policies

One of the most striking phenomena in the Asian region today is the structural reforms of the economy in the People's Republic of China (hereafter called China). Over the past few years, China has been trying to dissolve through ambitious reforms the centrally planned economic system which was solidly maintained over the previous three decades.

Like the Indian economy in the past, the Chinese economy under the centrally planned system with socialistic principles had been recognized as a typical high-cost economy in Asia. However, the rapid economic growth in neighboring Asian countries seems to have had considerable influence on the movement toward economic policy reforms in China. It was market-oriented and outward-looking policies that brought about high growth in the economies of the neighboring Asian countries. Their development stage and culture are not remote from, but are in fact quite similar to, that of China. Therefore the economic policies adopted in the neighboring countries have certainly provided China with a realistic model for its structural reforms.

The structural reforms in the Chinese economic system are comprised of three primary elements; namely, dissolution of the people's communes and promotion of individual farming in the agriculture sector, expansion of firms' self-autonomy in the industrial sector, and outward-looking policies. These three policies were launched after the Third Plenary Session of the 11th Central Committee Meeting of the Communist Party of China in 1978. The future of the Chinese economy as a whole can be seen through the remarkable flexibility shown by both the government and farmers in the policy reforms that were recently adopted in the agriculture sector. This topic is the focus of this chapter.

Agriculture in China had long been organized under the system of the people's communes. Although the system had been reshaped several times, it can be summarized as follows. A people's commune owned farm land, and the commune was responsible for achieving farm production targets and distributing production income among its farmers. Farmers cultivated the commune's land as planned by the commune and shared the products in accordance with their contribution. The communes developed irrigation facilities, established fertilizer plants, and owned large agricultural ma-

118

chines such as tractors. The people's communes consisted of a "three-tier ownership system." The commune was comprised of about ten to thirteen production brigades under which about eight production teams were formed, and each production team was made up of about thirty-one individual farms on average. The production team was directly involved in the day-to-day operations of individual farms. Farm land was, in practice, controlled by the production teams although, as was mentioned earlier, the farm land was the property of the commune. The team owned production means such as cattle and farm equipment. It was the production team who organized the farmers to achieve the production targets instructed by the commune headquarters and who distributed the production income among the farmers.

In terms of the distribution of income and food grain, under the general rule of the people's communes, an equitable distribution rule was adopted. No distinction was made in terms of rewards between hard and lazy workers. In order to determine the distribution of income among farmers, a labor point system was also introduced under which points were calculated on the basis of labor intensiveness multiplied by working hours. The labor point system later included the difference in the quality of labor among the farmers. However, measurement of labor intensiveness was determined on a case-by-case basis while judgement of labor quality tended to be subjective. Therefore, in the long run, it became a common tendency for farmers to try to waste a predetermined amount of time in the field with less labor intensiveness.

Since ancient times in China where population density was continuously high, "precise cultivation" in which labor was intensively employed in the whole process of farm production activities in order to maximize crop yields was the traditional means of agricultural production. Only through such traditional farming methods was it possible for China to more or less feed the gigantic population. Under the people's commune system, there were less incentives among farmers, and this resulted in careless farming in place of the traditional "precise cultivation." This naturally led to sluggish or no growth in agricultural productivity until after 1978.

While the land area of China looks extensive, the cultivable area is in fact much smaller. The cultivation ratio (i.e., the ratio of cultivable area to the total area) is presently only 11 percent which is far lower than the average in other Asian countries. A large part of the total land in China is occupied by such uncultivable areas as the Gobi desert, the Tibetan highlands, and other mountains. In addition to the low cultivation ratio, the forest ratio (i.e., ratio of forest area to the total area) is estimated to be 12.1 percent which is lower than the averages of 20.1 percent in Asia as a whole and 22.4 percent in the world. It should also be noted that agricultural productivity has decreased due to loss of land fertility which was caused by soil erosion mainly due to deforestation.

Cultivable land was so scarce in China that expansion of cultivable land was enthusiastically pursued by means of land reclamation. Through enormous "labor contribution without pay" under the commune system, barren areas were often transformed into cultivable land without due attention to ecological systems. However the cultivable area reached its maximum level of 111.83 million hectares in 1957 and since then it has followed a downward trend. It was, of course, possible to increase the land utilization rate through seasonal cropping, multicropping, and crop rotation. And, in fact, given its excessive population, China has actually been trying to maximize the land utilization rate together with continuous expansion of cultivable land. However, in view of the current agricultural technologies in China, it is difficult to increase the rate of land utilization much more than the current levels.

Taking into account its cultivation ratio as well as its cultivable land utilization rate, there is little room to expand the cropped area in China. Under these circumstances of scarcity of cultivable land, an increase in productivity can only be achieved by improving the farmers' full understanding of land scarcity and their intensive farming.

In the late 1970s, there was a growing tendency to adopt a proper incentive system under which farmers were guaranteed to receive higher rewards for harder work. Since 1978 when the Third Plenary Session of the Central Committee Meeting was held, an initial trial was embarked on to give more incentives to individual farmers who could increase agricultural productivity. Thus the collective farm management system has been gradually replaced by the farm-family management system.

What was Brought by the New Policy?

Following nationwide trials on a new approach to farm management called the "individual farm management contract system," the method was extensively adopted all over the country. By the end of 1983, this system had been adopted by more than 95 percent of all farms. The individual farm management contract system is as follows. An individual farmer rents out land from his production team through a contract. Then the farmer cultivates the land, taking care of crops with his own farm management efforts, and buying fertilizers, seeds, and farm equipment for his own use. When harvesting, a fixed share of his products must be delivered to his production team, and further deductions are made for agriculture taxes and for stockkeeping among his group in the production team. Then the remainder of the harvest belongs to himself, and can be sold freely in the market. This implies that individual farming management with self-autonomy has been revived.

Since almost all farmers adopted this system, the functions which used to belong to the people's communes have virtually faded away. During the period 1978 to 1984, 98 percent of the total number of people's communes were dissolved.

It should be emphasized here that the factor which led to the revival of the individual farming system was not initiated by the ideological reforms of the Central Communist Party but by the farmers' initiatives. It is believed that the major element which brought about changes in the agricultural policies rested with the farmers' strong demands for individual farm management. This obviously indicated that the past people's commune system did not work primarily because the system was a misguided concept influenced by excessive ideology.

The individual farm contract system was first introduced in Feng Yang prefecture in Anhui province. This method, which was originally considered to be an illegal practice, was publicly authorized by an executive of the Central Communist Party when he visited the province in 1979. As a result, the system expanded into neighboring areas and by 1983, 95 percent of all farms in China had adopted the individual farm contract system. Even in large rural areas where the people's commune systems had been firmly established, the individual farming system was rapidly revived within an unbelievably short period. Such speedy change could not be realized by means of only administrative measures from top to bottom; indeed this rapid adoption of the new system is adequate proof of the extent to which the Chinese farmers were willing to accept the changes and welcome the individual farming system.

At the same time that the individual farm contract system was introduced to provide incentives to farmers, another trial was initiated to increase crop production through an upward adjustment in government procurement prices for crops. Prices of not only food grain but also other crops and subsidiary crops were raised, while the prices of farm inputs, including farm implements, chemical fertilizers, and pesticides, were reduced. Thus the terms of trade for farm households (defined as the ratio of the comprehensive price index of farm households' sales to that of farm households' purchases) improved remarkably (Figure 10.1).

Due to the change in the farm management system from collective farming to individual farming on the one hand, and the considerable improvement in the terms of trade in favor of farmers on the other, farmers were greatly inspired to expand agricultural production and to increase agricultural productivity. Figure 10.2, which shows the trend of agricultural productivity expressed in terms of land and labor productivity, shows that land productivity has risen rapidly since 1978. In China where excessive labor always persisted, labor productivity had long been stagnant since a huge amount of

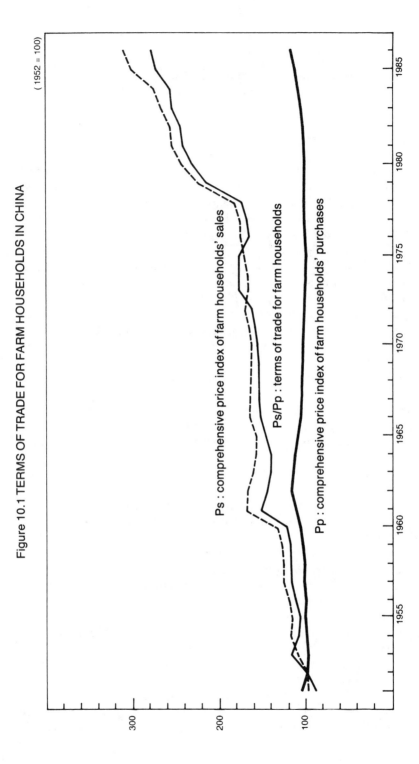

Figure 10.1 TERMS OF TRADE FOR FARM HOUSEHOLDS IN CHINA

(1952 = 100)

Ps : comprehensive price index of farm households' sales

Ps/Pp : terms of trade for farm households

Pp : comprehensive price index of farm households' purchases

SOURCE :   China, State Statistical Bureau. *Statistical Yearbook of China.* Beijing: SSB.

Figure 10.2 PRODUCTIVITY INDEX OF CHINESE AGRICULTURE

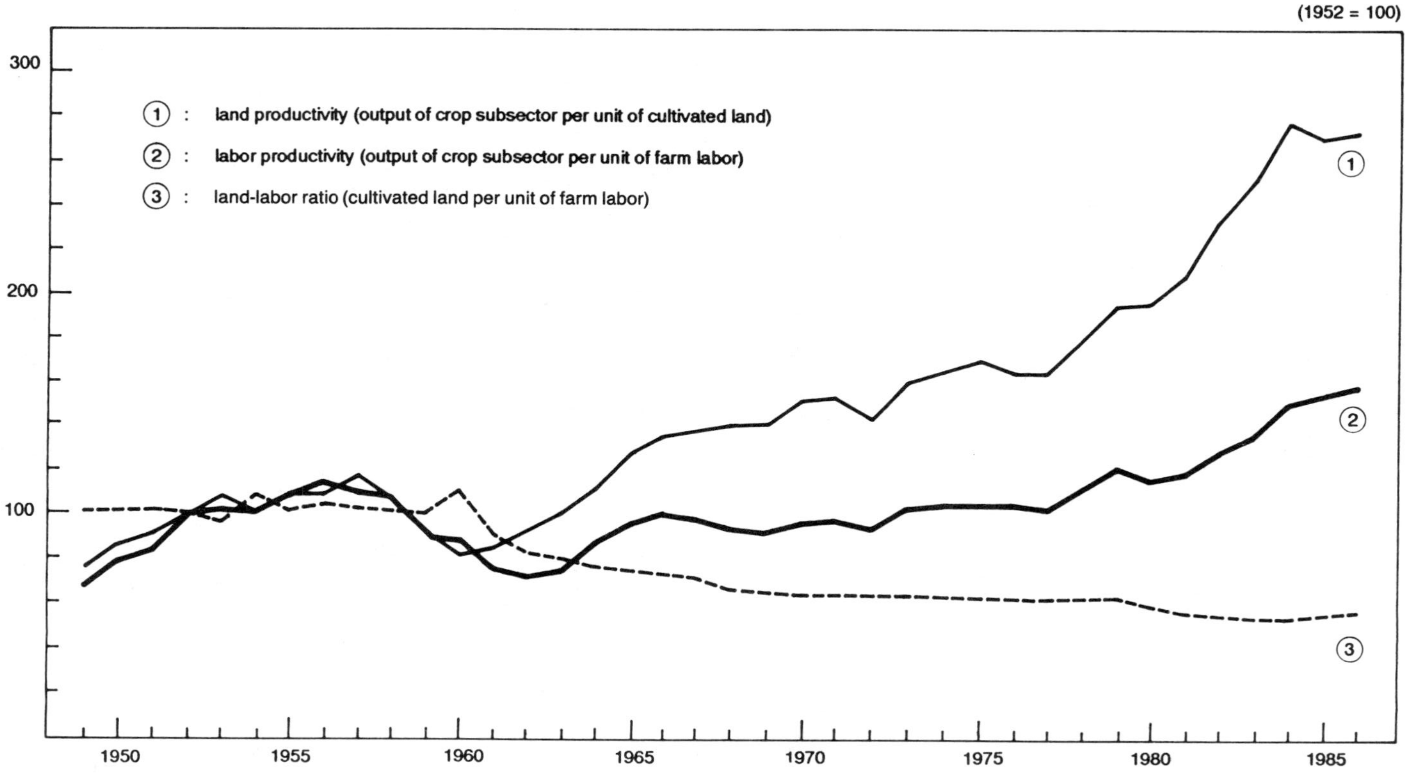
(1952 = 100)
300
200
100
① : land productivity (output of crop subsector per unit of cultivated land)
② : labor productivity (output of crop subsector per unit of farm labor)
③ : land-labor ratio (cultivated land per unit of farm labor)
1950
1955
1960
1965
1970
1975
1980
1985
①
②
③

SOURCE : China, State Statistical Bureau. *Statistical Yearbook of China.* Beijing: SSB.

Table 10.1

Agricultural Productivity in China

Q = agricultural output
R = cultivated land
L = labor force
Q/L = labor productivity (output per unit of labor force)
Q/R = land productivity (output per unit of cultivated area)
R/L = land-labor ratio (cultivated land per unit of labor)
$\quad Q/L = (Q/R) \times (R/L)$
$G(Q/L) = G(Q/R) + G(R/L)$
$\quad$ 1950–1977: 0.97% = 2.75% – 1.78%
$\quad$ 1977–1986: 5.46% = 7.17% – 1.71%

---

labor input had been spent on limited cultivable land. However, after 1978 labor productivity began to rise and followed an upward trend, entering into a higher range paralleling that of land productivity. Compared with 100 in the base year of 1952, the labor productivity index rose marginally to 103 in 1977 and reached 152 in 1985.

Using the same formula in Chapter 5, labor productivity in Chinese agriculture is compared over two different periods (Table 10.1). Between 1950 and 1977, a rise in land productivity was offset by the decrease in cultivated land per laborer, and this resulted in a low increase in labor productivity. However, from 1977 to 1986, labor productivity increased rapidly mainly due to a further rise in land productivity. Reflecting the increase in labor productivity, farm income, which was relatively stagnant before 1977, has also exhibited an upward trend since 1978 (Figure 10.3). This change in the trend was truly an epochal event.

So far our discussion has been confined to the crop production subsector of agriculture, which mainly includes food grains, oil seeds, canes, and other subsidiary crops such as beans. Obviously, food grain production plays a central role in agricultural development. Before 1978, the priority objective of the Chinese agriculture was to feed the huge population and the policy directives were concentrated towards the so-called first priority to food grain production. Little attention was paid to other agricultural activities including cash crops such as cotton, forestry, livestock, and fisheries. It is worth noting that since 1978 cash crops with a high return including cotton and hemp as well as other on-farm activities such as forestry, livestock, and fisheries have all expanded their production frontiers very rapidly. In addition, subsidiary off-farm enterprises have also expanded remarkably in rural areas.

The major subsidiary off-farm enterprises are rural industries. As indicated in Table 10.2, since 1978 the share of farm production in the value of total rural production decreased rapidly while the share of the rural industry

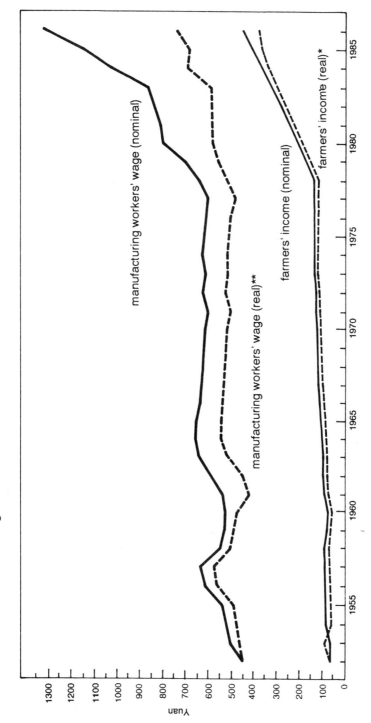

Figure 10.3 FARMERS' INCOME AND WORKERS' WAGE IN CHINA

manufacturing workers' wage (nominal)

manufacturing workers' wage (real)**

farmers' income (nominal)

farmers' income (real)*

Yuan

NOTES : *Deflated by comprehensive price index for farm households' purchases.
**Deflated by comprehensive price index for household consumption for staff and workers of the state-owned enterprises.

SOURCE : China, State Statistical Bureau. *Statistical Yearbook of China*. Beijing: SSB.

Table 10.2

Production Value by Economic Activity
in Rural Areas (percentage)

ECONOMIC ACTIVITY	1978	1986
Farm production	68.6	44.0
Rural industries	19.4	40.6
Rural construction works	6.6	8.3
Rural transportation	1.7	2.8
Rural merchandise and catering services	3.7	4.3
Total rural production	100.0	100.0

SOURCE: State Statistical Bureau. *Statistical Yearbook of China.*
Beijing: SSB.

increased significantly. A rapid rise in farm income levels after 1978 was mainly due to a rise in labor productivity in agricultural production, but also resulted from the rapid expansion of such nonagricultural production in rural areas.

As can be seen in Figure 10.4, where the farm income indexes are shown in relation to the share of nonagricultural production by province, agriculture in China, in conjunction with increased productivity, has made a big step towards diversification. As a successful result of the individual farm management contract system, capital surplus accumulated by progressive farmers was directed towards diversified economic activities which bear higher rates of return. The diversification is symbolized by the emergence of full-time specialized farms. Farmers who succeeded in saving capital started with various farm enterprises. They are full-time individual farmers who are specialized in such enterprises as cash crop production, pig farming and poultry, agro-processing factories such as oil and rice milling, repair and engineering services for farm equipment, transportation services, construction, merchandise, canteen services, and other rural off-farm businesses.

There is a growing tendency for these specialized farm enterprises to be integrated into larger well-organized enterprises. They are called *xiang zhen* (township) enterprises; *xiang* means a unit of village administration while *zhen* means a small city in rural areas. *Xiang zhen* are entrepreneurship coalitions among specialized farm enterprises which have already acquired self-autonomy in management. They are allied to each other in seeking much higher returns from their accumulated capital. These enterprises are now rapidly growing in the field of manufacturing.

The number of *xiang zhen* enterprises mushroomed after the Third Plenary Session of the 11th Central Committee Meeting of the Communist Party of China in 1978. During this session, significant changes in agricul-

Figure 10.4 RATIO OF NONAGRICULTURAL INCOME TO FARMERS' INCOME IN CHINA, 1985

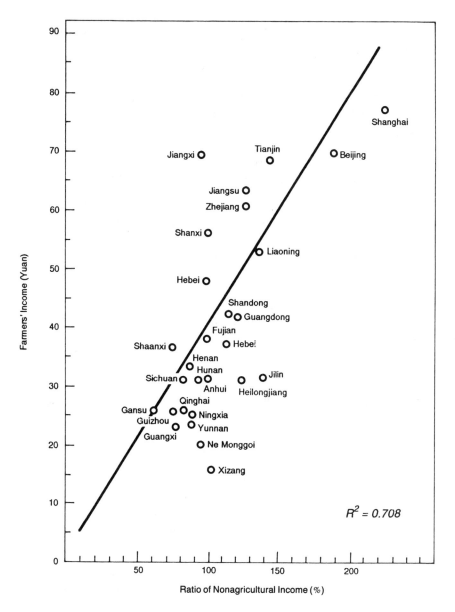

NOTE :   Ratio of nonagricultural income = (income from nonagricultural production)/(farmers' income). National average = 100.

SOURCE :   China, State Statistical Bureau. *Statistical Yearbook of China*. Beijing: SSB.

tural policy were made. The increase in agricultural productivity arising from these changes in policy brought about a capital surplus in farm households on the one hand, and revealed a labor surplus in rural areas on the other. This labor surplus (underemployment or disguised unemployment) was further revealed when the movement of farm labor to nonagricultural activities in rural areas was deregulated. Both the money and labor surpluses that were induced by the changes in agricultural policies were absorbed by the *xiang zhen* enterprises, resulting in the explosive expansion of these enterprises in rural areas.

The *xiang zhen* enterprises were established on the basis of a new management style in which they could freely produce and sell their products without public interventions. Their productivity and profitability are much higher than that of farms, partly because rural areas have been suffering from a perpetual shortage of light industrial goods and high prices of commodities. Therefore, farmers have been continuously investing their surplus money and labor in *xiang zhen*. It has been estimated that between 1978 and 1986, 180 billion yuan was transferred from the agricultural to the nonagricultural sector, mainly to *xiang zhen* enterprises in rural areas. During the same period, the nonagricultural sector absorbed 79 million laborers from the agricultural sector. Subtracting the 22 million laborers in rural areas that had already been employed by rural enterprises which were predecessors of *xiang zhen* enterprises, this means that 57 million laborers were employed by the nonagricultural sector within only eight years. This represents about 70 percent of the total number of laborers that were absorbed by all enterprises owned by communes over the period 1952–1986; this is a truly remarkable achievement of the private sector's initiatives.

Soon after their establishment, the *xiang zhen* increased their contribution to the Chinese economy. The share of these enterprises in the total production value of agriculture and industry rapidly increased, reaching 23.4 percent in 1986. In 1985 the total value of output from the *xiang zhen* enterprises exceeded the total value of output from the agricultural sector, and accounted for about 18 percent of total export earnings.

Further expansion of the *xiang zhen* enterprises and a further increase in the absorptive capacity of labor in these enterprises are the most important single factor to keep in mind when considering how the Chinese economy could establish an integrated relationship between the two sectors (namely, the agriculture and industrial sectors) and to what extent the economy will contribute in creating a new dimension of spiral mechanism in the development process.

As described above, the new agricultural policies since 1978 deprived people's communes of their role in agricultural production and led to the revival of individual farming. Furthermore, new pricing measures were introduced to provide enough incentives to increase agricultural production and to diversify the rural production base. This resulted in a dramatic increase in rural productivity and income. These were the major changes brought about by the new policies since 1978.

Changes in the Pattern of Capital Accumulation

There is no doubt that China is still an agricultural country. Therefore the reforms may well be recognized as changes in the fundamental basis of the Chinese economy. Indeed, the policy reforms observed in the agriculture sector in the past decade have induced fundamental changes in the development mechanism of the Chinese economy as a whole.

Before 1978 the Chinese economy was in a stage of "high accumulation pattern" in which high industrial growth was envisaged by means of resource transfers from agriculture to heavy industry through maximization of the surplus gained in the agricultural sector. The government procured agricultural produce at a low price from farmers and sold the produce at only a slightly higher price to the light industry sectors which were nationally owned and operated. The goods manufactured in these factories including fertilizer, farm equipment, and consumer goods were, in turn, sold to farmers and laborers at a higher price through nationally managed enterprises. This resulted in excessive profit for nationally owned factories and enterprises; this profit was, through taxes on industry and commerce, absorbed into the national treasury which comprised a large portion of national revenues. Abundant revenue that was collected in this manner was largely invested in the heavy industry sector consisting mainly of the steel industry (the popular slogan was "steel is essential for everything"). This explains why China has achieved a rate of heavy industrialization that is higher than other developing countries. (This will be discussed further in the next chapter.)

However, under the new agricultural policies, the Chinese economy was forced to change this strategy of financing industrialization. Due to the increased procurement prices for agricultural produce and the reduced prices for agricultural inputs, the agricultural sector could no longer act as a source of funding for capital formation in the industrial sector. The persistent deficit in the national budget in these years is largely due to the increase in procurement prices for agricultural produce. Particularly in 1983, a gap between the high procurement prices and low release prices grew to such an extent that the government's expenditure to fill the gap exceeded more than 30 percent of the total recurrent budget of the country. It may be said that the agricultural sector had now turned into a "protected industry." The past high accumulation pattern in which the savings were persistently sought from the agricultural sector had come to an end, and the agricultural surplus which was compulsorily "extracted" through the system of the people's communes did not occur. Since it became difficult to obtain savings from the agricultural sector, the industrial sector itself has had to find a new source for funding further capital formation.

As the Chinese industrial sector is obliged to find a source of savings, it has had to exploit its own potential resources as well as pursue efficient operations through reforms in the systems of industrial management. It is, therefore, logical for policy reforms in the industrial sector to focus mainly on the delegation of management autonomy to manufacturing enterprises. Following a reasonable length of time after the reform of the agriculture sector, industrial policy reforms are now ready to be implemented. The industrial sector reforms which are recognized as another pillar of the overall economic reforms in China as well as the outward-looking policies will be discussed in the next chapter.

CHAPTER ELEVEN

Enterprise Reforms and an Outward-Looking Strategy in China

High-Cost Economies

As was noted in the previous chapter, remarkable progress has been made in the agricultural sector in China. China, the largest socialist country in Asia, succeeded in achieving a substantial increase in productivity and income in this sector. This was accomplished through decisive policy changes in the centrally planned economic system which had been firmly established for several decades in China. But what has happened in the industrial sector? The answer is that the industrial sector is also decontrolling the socialist regulations that prevailed under the planned economy, and is gradually introducing the mechanisms of a market-oriented economy. This chapter will discuss how this process is progressing.

Before discussing the topic, let us briefly review the history of China's industrialization since its independence. As shown in Figure 11.1, a salient characteristic of the Chinese economy lies in the fact that the investment rate in China (i.e., the ratio of the aggregated amount of investment over the total value of national product) was substantially higher than in other developing countries. Empirically, the tendency is that the lower the per capita income, the lower the investment rate. In this context, China was an exceptional case indeed.

The reason for the investment rate being so high in China lay in the country's ambitious undertakings in heavy industry despite the fact that China still remained one of the low-income countries. As shown in Figure 11.2, while the ratio of investment in heavy industry to the total amount of investment has remained at around 50 percent for a long time, the ratio of investment in heavy industry to total investment in the industrial sector has been much higher at about 90 percent. In no other country has there been such a high concentration of investment in the heavy industry sector. Figure 11.3 provides a comparison of heavy industrialization rates between China and South Korea. South Korea is well known as one of the developing countries in which rapid heavy industrialization has been achieved since the early 1970s. By 1986, there was a very wide gap in per capita income between the two—US$300 for China and US$2,370 for Korea. Notwithstanding this, the

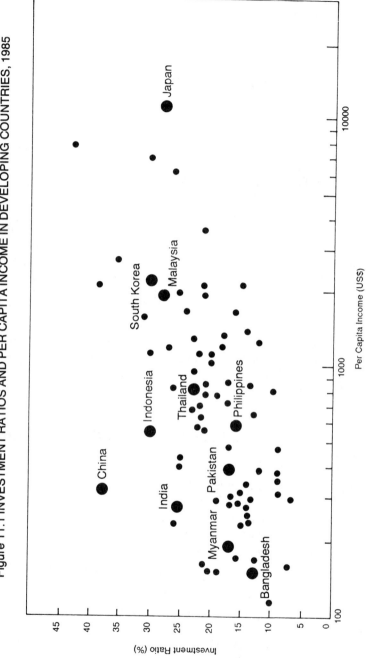

Figure 11.1 INVESTMENT RATIOS AND PER CAPITA INCOME IN DEVELOPING COUNTRIES, 1985

SOURCE : World Bank. *World Development Report.* Washington, D.C.: WB.

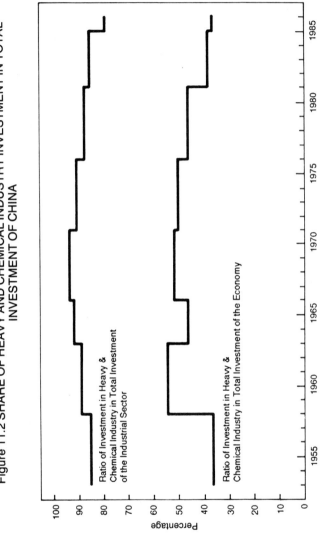

Figure 11.2 SHARE OF HEAVY AND CHEMICAL INDUSTRY INVESTMENT IN TOTAL INVESTMENT OF CHINA

Ratio of Investment in Heavy & Chemical Industry in Total Investment of the Industrial Sector

Ratio of Investment in Heavy & Chemical Industry in Total Investment of the Economy

Percentage

SOURCE : China, State Statistical Bureau. *Statistical Yearbook of China*. Beijing: SSB.

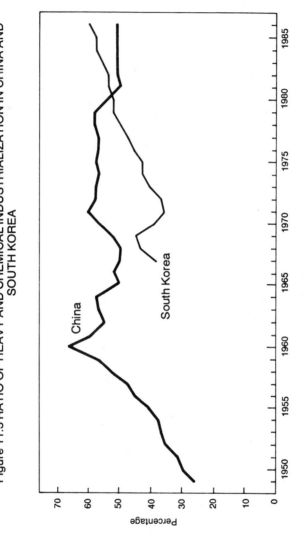

Figure 11.3 RATIO OF HEAVY AND CHEMICAL INDUSTRIALIZATION IN CHINA AND SOUTH KOREA

NOTE : Ratios of heavy and chemical industrialization is defined as the ratio of the output value of machinery, metal and chemical industries to the total output value of all manufacturing industries at constant prices.

SOURCE : China, State Statistical Bureau. *Statistical Yearbook of China.* Beijing: SSB.

rate of heavy industrialization in China had been higher than that of South Korea until 1980.

Given China's poor economic environment, a rapid increase in investment was a logical step to realizing faster economic modernization. Unfortunately though, it appears that the Chinese industrialization process in the past was unbelievably inefficient. In the case of capitalist economies, every enterprise has to monitor market movement all the time, and then increase its investment only when the probability of making a profit from the investment is reasonably certain. Furthermore, under capitalist economies, each individual enterprise must make every effort to increase efficiency with the aim of reducing the output price as well as the costs of production, as it has to operate in severe competition with other enterprises. In contrast, in the centrally planned economies, every possible effort is devoted to achieving targets given by the higher authority while market trends and increases in efficiency in production are often ignored. Industrialization efforts in China have been affected by this inherent deficiency for a long time.

Around 1980, it was widely reported that one-third of the total production capacity of the industrial sector in China was idle. Furthermore, one-third of all state enterprises were obliged to operate at a financial loss. At that time, the capacity of crude steel production was 55 million mt per year, while the actual annual production amounted to only 32 million mt; this implies that there was an unbelievably high level of excess capacity to produce 13 million mt of crude steel. The example of the steel industry is just one indication that the process of Chinese industrialization was extremely inefficient.

The high level of inefficiency in China can also be shown using economic terminology by which efficiency of economic management is measured. The marginal output-capital ratio indicates what percentage of production is brought about by a one percentage increase in investment. The ratios of the Asian countries are shown in Table 11.1. The table indicates the relatively low output-capital ratio in China in the past. It is important to discuss what factors made the Chinese industrialization so inefficient and what measures are being pursued by the Chinese economy in order to rectify the persistent inefficiency.

Before 1978, many factories were directly controlled by the highly centralized administration, and they were not allowed to have managerial autonomy in running their own factories. Within the internal organization of a certain individual factory, a branch of the communist party was created; the branch secretary, who was ranked above the factory manager, directly supervised the factory operations with guidance from the Central Party. Production targets to be achieved by factories were given by the higher authority without detailed consultations, and the enterprises were expected only to

Table 11.1
Index of Investment Efficiency
in Selected Asian Countries[a]

COUNTRY	1960–1970	1970–1980
China	0.28[b]	–
Hong Kong	0.48	0.37
Indonesia	0.35	0.39
Malaysia	0.36	0.30
Philippines	0.25	0.22
Singapore	0.38	0.21
South Korea	0.37	0.31
Taiwan	0.39	0.31
Thailand	0.36	0.28

NOTES: a. The index is defined as $G(Y)/G(K)$ where $G(Y)$ is a marginal increase in production while $G(K)$ is a marginal increase in capital stock. Thus, the index means the percentage increase in production that is induced by a one percentage increase in capital stock, which indicates efficiency in investment.

b. 1953–1978.

SOURCE: Kawachi, S., A. Fujimoto, and H. Ueno. 1987. *Henbo Suru Chugoku Keizai* [*Changing economies in China*]. Sekai Shiso Sha: Tokyo.

achieve the targets faithfully. All the necessary inputs to achieve the instructed targets, including raw materials, energy, machinery and equipment, and even wages for labor, were distributed by the higher authority. At the same time, a procedure was adopted in which products manufactured by factories were mostly handed over to the higher authority for marketing. The number and qualifications of laborers needed for production could not be decided upon by the factories themselves, but were dictated by the higher authority. This meant that the factories could not execute their own personnel management policies. Further, the factories were not permitted to keep any of the profit. A factory manager was directly supervised by the Party Committee, and he acted only as a faithful representative of the higher authority's will. This represents a typical example of the centrally planned economic system. In fact, this system was introduced on the basis of "the wartime communist supply model" prevailing in the Soviet Union in the 1920s.

The communist supply model could be effective in ensuring the supply of indispensable goods during the emergency wartime period. However, its inherent deficiencies become obvious if such a production and delivery system is adopted under normal conditions.

Under the communist supply system, it is not possible to expect entrepreneurship behavior under which efficient production is always pursued to maximize profit. Continuous efforts to improve management efficiency, which was a key concept among enterprises in capitalist economies, was completely lacking in industrial development in China and factories were allowed to survive in China regardless of efficiency. If a factory was well managed and there resulted a net surplus from the improvement in managerial efficiency, the profit was absorbed by the higher authority; in the case of a deficit, the loss was covered by the higher authority. Furthermore, fixed wages were paid both to the factory manager and unskilled workers, and they were completely free from the risk of being laid off. It may be concluded, therefore, that there was little incentive for industrial enterprises to improve their efficiency in production.

Moreover, many troubles arose because of poor and ineffective coordination among the higher authorities. There were many cases where coordination was lacking between a section instructing production targets, a section dealing with distribution of inputs and energy, and a section responsible for marketing. The lack of coordination often resulted in underachievement of production targets due to the lack of inputs and energy. Serious shortages in supply or the grave situation of excessive stocks also occurred often.

Even so, the deficiencies of the system cannot be rectified simply by strengthening the coordination capacity of the administrative machinery or by streamlining the decision-making machinery. The Chinese economy, which is large in size and complicated in nature, is not so simple that it can be controlled by human intellect alone. It seems true that the various problems resulted essentially from the inherent deficiency of the centrally planned economic system itself rather than from the specific deficiency in the practice of economic management in China. It may be said that the huge and complicated economy in China can be controlled only by "invisible hands" through market mechanisms. What is going on in contemporary China is that instead of improving or streamlining the old economic systems, they have enthusiastically embarked on introducing market mechanisms in order to overcome the deficiencies observed in the centrally planned economic system of the past decades. It may be concluded, therefore, that China has, after a long period of trial and error, come to understand the principles of a market economy.

Extension of Enterprise Autonomy

Although many reforms in the industrial sector are still only half implemented, several decisive changes have been made. These changes look unbelievably innovative, particularly for people who have observed the rigid economic systems of the past and that operated under the socialist regimes.

Table 11.2

Provisional Guidelines for Expansion of Public Enterprise Autonomy
in China, May 1984

1. An enterprise can produce goods at its discretion once it achieves the target previously contracted with the State.
2. Products, if these are not the commodities regulated by the State, can be sold on the open market.
3. Prices of goods sold on the open market can be set within a 20 percent range of the guiding prices.
4. An enterprise can choose suppliers at its discretion.
5. Seventy percent of depreciation funds can be retained by enterprises.
6. Fixed capital which is not used by a certain enterprise can be rented out or sold.
7. An enterprise can decide its organizational and personnel matters at its discretion.
8. A factory superintendent is appointed by the higher authority while the deputy superintendent and other staff are appointed by the superintendent.
9. An enterprise can decide its own wage scheme, and the superintendent is authorized to determine incentives including wage increases and bonus payments.
10. An enterprise can participate in integrated corporations beyond sectors and regions.

the various industrial reforms that have been carried out since 1978, "provisional instructions for further expansion of the autonomy of state enterprises" promulgated by the Bureau of National Affairs in May 1984 was recognized as one of the epoch-making reforms in the industrial sector. Major points of the reforms, which are summarized in Table 11.2, point to the introduction of market mechanisms and the expansion of self-autonomy for state enterprises. The first, second, and third items in the table show that: (1) the regulated share of produce to be purchased by the government may be reduced, (2) the remaining portion to be sold by enterprises may be increased, and (3) the selling price shall be set in line with market prices. The fourth item indicates that production inputs and energy distributed by the government at low fixed prices may be reduced while the portion of inputs purchased by enterprises themselves at market prices may be increased. Furthermore, self-autonomy was widely given to enterprises with regards to management, including personnel and organizational control.

In the past, a factory superintendent of a Chinese enterprise acted as a puppet that was following instructions given from its higher authority, and he merely tried to attain the production targets given by the authority. Problems arose as the authority had little experience and knowledge about factory management and production. However, factory superintendents have recently been given greater responsibility in managing their enterprises so that they are now recognized as key decision makers in improving management efficiency in the production process. At the same time, it now becomes possible for the enterprises to determine the wage level of workers; in the past, the wage level was widely fixed at uniform rates in accordance with job classification and grade of labor intensity. Furthermore, the responsibility of enterprises has been expanded with regards to personnel management so that the enterprises are now able to pursue efficiency in employment management. A worker contract system has recently been introduced; under this system, enterprises can work out contracts with workers that cover the rights and obligations of both parties. This implies that managerial autonomy over employment policy has been given to the enterprises.

Profit making forms an essential part of enterprise management. The recent rapid increase in profit reserves within enterprises is important in view of the long-term growth of the manufacturing sector. After a series of different regulations that have been in place since 1978, the latest set of rules has guaranteed that enterprises can retain their entire profits after paying taxes. Through this tax policy, the financial status of enterprises has become much stronger than before.

The expansion of enterprises' autonomy has caused a chain effect on other aspects of institutional systems. Along with the liberalization of the purchase of production inputs and energy by enterprises as well as of the increased share of their produce to be sold on the open market, open market systems, the importance of which is now widely recognized, are now emerging rapidly. At the same time, the expansion of enterprise autonomy has brought about an increased demand for working capital as well as for efficiency in enterprise management. To meet these requirements, the rationalization of the banking and financial systems is now being pursued. Once enterprises rely on borrowing from banks which require repayment of interest and principal, they have to behave as real enterprises in the true meaning of the word. They also have to be guided by the primary policy of entrepreneurship, namely, continuous improvement in managerial efficiency in production. As mentioned above, the expansion of enterprise autonomy has induced a series of institutional reforms relating to enterprise management. The sequential pattern of "liberalization induces further liberalization" is now whirling in China.

Intention of the Open Economies

The liberalization policies are being further accelerated by overseas-oriented economic policies. A salient feature of the recently adopted policies is the establishment of four special economic zones in which substantial economic freedom is given. In 1980, an ordinance for establishing the special economic zones was issued in Guandong province, which was followed by the creation

Table 11.3

Outline of Administrative Order for The Shenzhen Special Economic Zone

---

1. Full management autonomy is given to an enterprise which is established by a foreign investor.
2. Management autonomy is usually given to joint or corporate enterprises, and the public administration in the economic specialized zones may not intervene in their activities through administrative orders.
3. Enterprises can, when they recruit staff and laborers, select them on the basis of individual examination.
4. Enterprises may apply a force-account wage system, a variable wage system, or a wage scale by skill grades.
5. Prices in the specialized zones are, in principle, guided by market mechanism.
6. Enterprise income tax is fixed at 15 percent which is lower than in Hong Kong. Tax holiday of 1–3 years or 20–50 percent less income tax may be given to enterprises whose investment is more than US$5 million or whose preparatory period is long due to sophisticated technology. In the event that profit made by the foreign investors is reinvested within the specialized zones, income tax on the profit may be reduced on request.
7. Import duty may be exempted when capital goods and consumer goods are imported into the specialized zones.
8. Export tax on products produced in the specialized zones may be exempted.
9. The specialized zones may provide land to foreign investors on a priority basis, and rent should be much less expensive than in Hong Kong.
10. Products are mainly for export, but the share for the domestic market can be adequately determined in accordance with domestic and international demand for the products.

SOURCE: 1984. *Beijing Chou Pao,* No. 4.

of three additional special zones at Shenzhen, Zhuhai, and Shantou. This was further extended to other special zones at Amoy in Fujiang province (Figure 11.4). As shown by the major features of the institutional arrangements and administrative regulations (Table 11.3), the government intended to invite many foreign enterprises by providing adequate incentives and maximum freedom in pursuing their business activities.

In 1984, fourteen coastal cities and Hainan island were institutionalized as economic development zones and were given the same degree of freedom as the special economic zones. Furthermore, a bold experimental scheme is being considered to expand the special economic or development zones to a whole province and/or a certain deltaic area of a river. It is the government's intention to use these special economic zones and economic development zones as a window to introduce foreign capital, technology, and modern enterprise management systems.

The establishment of the special economic zones and special economic development zones is expected to make the return of Hong Kong and Taiwan smoother. Hong Kong is now acting as the largest window for Chinese

Figure 11.4 LOCATION OF ECONOMICALLY OPEN AREAS IN CHINA

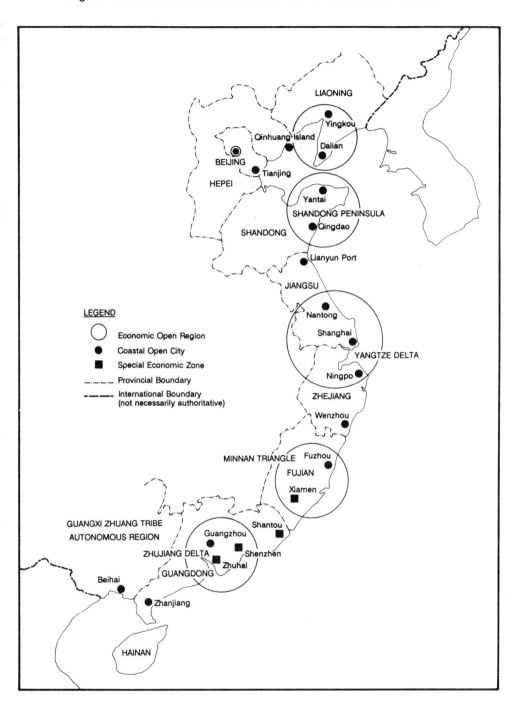

trade and the most important source of foreign exchange earnings. Hong Kong, which acts as one of the international financing centers, has the various resources necessary for economic modernization including management skill of modern enterprises, skilled labor, and advanced technologies. It would be natural for the Chinese government, which is seeking rapid economic modernization, to want to bring into its territory the resources similar to those that exist in Hong Kong.

In other words, the Chinese government intends to encourage joint ventures with foreign enterprises in special economic zones and development zones by which capital from industrialized countries, Hong Kong, Taiwan, and overseas Chinese in Southeast Asia can be mobilized. At the same time, China's enterprises intend to establish joint ventures with those of Hong Kong through the transfer of capital from mainland China. The authoritative return of Hong Kong to China in 1997 without the provision of economic interaction between the two (which would generate mutual benefits) may be harmful to both sides. Therefore, the Chinese government has advocated that Hong Kong be kept as it is and that it should, in principle, be governed by the Hong Kong people themselves. By doing so, the Chinese government hopes to convince the Hong Kong people and the overseas Chinese, and to realize "expanded Hong Kong" in its territory. As a matter of fact, three economic special zones were established in Guangdong and one in Fujiang from where most of the overseas Chinese came to Southeast Asia. Shenzhen is near Hong Kong while Zhukai is close to the border with Macao. The location of Amoy seems to be symbolical as it faces Taiwan.

New Directions Envisaged by the Outward-Looking Strategy

It seems that China's outward-looking policies have already reached a stage where setbacks are impossible. A new strategy aimed at expansion of labor-intensive manufacturing products is the only path that is left for Chinese industrialization. This strategy intends to resolve various contradictions that emerged during the decade of reforms since 1978 and to explore alternative paths for the future. *Economic Development Strategy in the Coastal Areas,* which was issued in January 1988 by Mr. Zhao Xi Yang, will undoubtably play a key role in the development strategy of China in the near future. The logic of why China had to adopt an economic growth strategy in the coastal areas is discussed below.

As mentioned earlier, the most vital economic units under the period of structural reforms since 1978 were *xiang zhen* enterprises. Without the huge labor-absorptive capability of these *xiang zhen* enterprises, the persistent problem of excess labor in China could not be eradicated. A review of the successful performances of these enterprises in the past decade may naturally lead one to expect them to make a further contribution to the Chinese economy. Indeed, it is believed that there is still potential for further growth in *xiang zhen* enterprises, but it will be necessary for them to be equipped with additional capital.

However, along with the economic vitalization, there has emerged a serious shortage of infrastructure, including energy supply and transportation. As shown in Figure 11.5, while national income has increased rapidly since 1978, energy supply and cargo traffic volume have not kept pace. This may indicate a grave bottleneck caused by inadequate provision of such infrastructure in China. At present, the shortage of electricity supply has become serious to the extent that about 20 to 30 percent of the factories in the country are idle, and about 30 percent of the urban population and 40 percent of

Figure 11.5 BOTTLENECKS IN TRANSPORT AND ENERGY SECTORS IN CHINA

(1978 = 100)

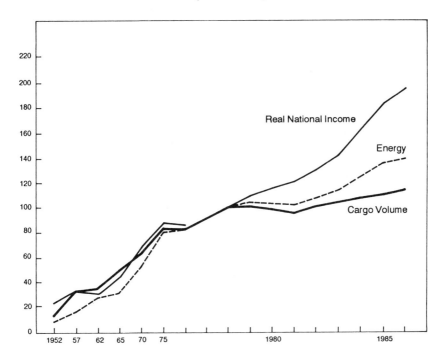

NOTE :   Energy is estimated at standard coal equivalent while cargo volume is estimated in terms of ton/km.

SOURCE :   China, State Statistical Bureau. *Statistical Yearbook of China*. Beijing: SSB.

Table 11.4

Comparison of Transport Capacities between
China and India

	CHINA	INDIA
	1981	1986
Km per 1,000 persons		
Railway	0.05	0.09
Roads	0.91	2.43
Km per 1,000 Sq. km (density)		
Railway	6	19
Roads	93	488
	1985	1980
Cargo (mt per km)		
Railway	8,216	1,965
Passengers (persons per km)		
Railway	2,416	2,396

SOURCE: Azia Keizai Kenkyujo [Institute of Developing Economies]. 1988. *Higashi Azia Shokoku no Keizai Kaihatsu Keikaku to Waga Kuni Keizai Kyoryoku no Arikata* [*Economic development plans in east Asian countries and Japanese economic cooperation*]. Tokyo: IDE.

the rural population have no access to electricity. Lack of transportation is also an increasingly serious problem. Demand for transportation has increased along with the increased transactions among regional economic zones (where self-sufficiency was established) that resulted from the economic vitalization. Thus, lack of transportation facilities will be a major constraint in the future economic growth of China. Table 11.4 illustrates how the Chinese transportation (roads and railways) systems are poor in comparison with those of India. Obviously excess demand for transportation exists in China, which implies the overutilization of the existing transport capacity.

A large amount of capital is required to remove the bottleneck in infrastructure. However, the high accumulation pattern which had been realized by squeezing agricultural surplus under the commune system has been abandoned. In fact, the current accumulation ratio, excluding foreign capital inflows, is at its lowest level.

Notwithstanding the fact that domestic accumulation is continuing to shrink, the Chinese economy requires additional capital for *xiang zhen* enterprises in order to provide them with adequate facilities. This investment aims at absorbing the excess labor force from the agricultural sector into the industrial sector. At the same time, the Chinese economy must improve its infrastructure including energy supply and transportation. China has reached a phase in which these two requirements, which demand a huge amount of capital, must be satisfied at the same time. However, allocation of domestic resources to these two requirements is becoming increasingly difficult. This is the primary dilemma that contemporary China is facing.

To solve this dilemma, Wang Jian presented an article (his development scenario formed the basis of the above mentioned report of Zhao Xi Yang) which concluded that by promoting the labor-intensive–cum–export-oriented industrialization, surplus labor in rural areas would be absorbed in the sector on the one hand, and the heavy industry and infrastructure sectors would be developed by the reallocation of foreign exchange resources earned by the exports on the other.

> Migration of the rural labor force should be incorporated into the international circulation system. Namely, it is a logical consequence that increased production of labor intensive products for export can resolve the current problem of excessive labor surplus in rural areas, and at the same time earn foreign exchange in the international market. Foreign exchange represents all kinds of resources. Once abundant foreign exchange becomes available, capital and technology needed for the development of heavy industry can be obtained. Through active participation in the international market, the domestic interaction between the agriculture and the heavy industry sectors can be further strengthened, and such interaction may be one of preconditions for resolving the current contradictions in the domestic economy. (Wang Churn. 1988. Choose A Right Long-Term Development Strategy. *Jing Chie Ripao*, January 5)

The economic development strategy in coastal areas that was advocated by Zhao Xi Yang provided a means of implementing Wang's theory. Zhao expected *xiang zhen* enterprises in coastal areas to be responsible for exporting labor-intensive processed goods that are made of imported materials. That is, labor-intensive enterprises in coastal areas were to import raw materials and export the value-added goods to international markets. This strategy was meant to avoid possible conflict with the domestic economy in obtaining scarce domestic resources. In short, the manufacturing enterprises in the coastal areas have to operate both ends of the production process overseas; namely, importing of raw materials and exporting of processed goods. Another striking strategy is the promotion of foreigners' investment in terms of 100-percent foreign investment enterprises, joint investment enterprises, and cooperated enterprises. Through the participation of foreign investment, the *xiang zhen* enterprises intend to improve the quality of their products, upgrade technological standards, improve firm management, and secure the marketing of their products overseas.

Ever since they were born, township enterprises have been responsible for their own financial outcome in terms of profit or loss. They were brought up in an open market where competition prevailed. They can grow up if they are competitive, while they have to either close down or seek other business if they are not competitive. Competition among themselves for survival is quite intense. They are flexible in management, small in scale, quick in response, efficient in services, and reliable in time-bound contracts. Foreign trading corporations are eager to have business with township enterprises. Most township enterprises have little surplus of labor, and they fully utilize their production capacities. As they are exposed to intense market competition, township enterprises are, in general, keen to improve technology and to develop new products. The forward-looking attitude of township enterprises is a significant advantage in the production of export goods, and this is suitable not only for competition in the domestic market but also in the international market.

In the past few years, township enterprises have grown up rapidly, and have been organized into large groups. They are in full swing in Zhujiang delta, Yangtze delta, Shandong peninsula, and Liaodong peninsula. Although many township enterprises started with minimum capital and facilities, they are now considerably different from what they were at the beginning. In Wujiang in Suzhou city, I have seen a textile factory which procured advanced machinery from Switzerland. There are many newly built factories in the area. Buildings and facilities of township enterprises are not always shabby in comparison with nationalized factories. The share of township enterprises in the total export earnings in the coastal areas has increased tremendously. Township enterprises have been oriented to develop labor intensive products for export, and they have successfully put the coastal areas right on the overseas trade map. They are now recognized as active promoters for foreign exchange earnings through exports. (1988. Economic Development Strategy for Coastal Areas Told by Zhao Xi Yang. *Renmin Ripao,* December 23)

This outward-looking strategy fits with the current trade and investment climate that has prevailed on the basis of the structural changes rapidly emerging in the Western Pacific region (which will be discussed in the next chapter). Owing to the strong yen, Japan has become a huge importing country, and Japanese enterprises are transferring their production bases to countries in the Western Pacific region. Even South Korea and Taiwan are losing their comparative advantages in labor-intensive industries, and they are also increasingly shifting their production bases to less developed countries in the Western Pacific region. Economic relations between China and South Korea and China and Taiwan are maturing. The investment climate to promote the export-oriented–cum–labor-intensive industries in the coastal areas in China seems to be encouraging. China seems to have decided to participate in the Western Pacific market through internationalization of *xiang zhen* enterprises in the coastal areas together with the introduction of foreign capital and technology. The economic growth strategy in the coastal areas reflects the long-term perspectives of the Chinese government, which has as one of its goal the utilization of the development dynamism prevailing in the Western Pacific region into its economy.

It is interesting to see how China will succeed in realizing sustained growth in the national economy by adopting the wave of industrialism that is whirling in the neighboring countries, and through the introduction of market mechanisms and outward-looking policies. It is also interesting to see to what extent the empirical experiences of Japan and the Asian NIEs will be effective in China. For the people who are interested in economic development in Asia, it seems that a gigantic drama has just started in China.

CHAPTER TWELVE

The Era of the Western Pacific

Challenges and Counter-Challenges

The center of gravity in the modern civilization of industrial technology is shifting from the Atlantic region to the Pacific region, especially to the countries located on the western rim of the Pacific Ocean. The Asian NIEs started their economic growth in the early 1960s and have recorded the highest growth in the world since that time and through the 1980s. Growth of the ASEAN economies accelerated during the 1970s, while the world economy experienced severe setbacks due to the two oil crises. China, with its huge economic potential, also started to move forward in the late 1970s. Among the generally weakened industrialized economies, Japan continues to maintain its exceptional vigor.

In the stagnating world economy, these Western Pacific countries are demonstrating exceptional economic strength. They truly deserve the name of "the growing region." Judging from their growth potential, the region will probably play a leading role in world economic growth in the future. This chapter gives a brief overview of the economic dynamism found in the Western Pacific.

The high economic growth of this region has been led by industrialization. Within a relatively short period of time, the countries in the region have rapidly built up their industrial production capacities. As shown in Table 12.1, the share of manufacturing output in GDP has increased sharply in the past quarter of the century. In 1986, manufacturing output accounted for 21 to 39 percent of GDP in the Asian NIEs and 18 to 25 percent in all of the ASEAN countries except Indonesia. In contrast, the average share of manufacturing output in the industrialized countries was 23 percent. This shows the high level of industrialization that has been attained by the Asian NIEs and ASEAN countries.

Growth of industrial production capacities in these countries resulted in the reinforcement of their export capacities in the following years. As shown in Table 12.2, both Japan and the Asian NIEs have significantly increased their share of world exports and imports. However, the share of the Asian NIEs increased much faster than Japan's. Nine countries in the Western Pacific Region—namely, the Asian NIEs, the ASEAN countries, and Japan —have increased their combined share of world exports from 8.4 percent in

Table 12.1
Structure of Production in Selected Asia-Pacific Countries

COUNTRY	AGRICULTURE 1960	AGRICULTURE 1986	INDUSTRY[a] 1960	INDUSTRY[a] 1986	MANUFACTURING 1960	MANUFACTURING 1986	SERVICES 1960	SERVICES 1986
Hong Kong	4	0	39	29	26	21	57	71
Indonesia	54	26	14	32	8	14	32	42
Malaysia	36	23	18	30	9	18	45	47
Philippines	26	26	28	32	20	25	46	42
Singapore	4	1	18	37	12	27	78	62
South Korea	37	12	20	42	14	30	43	45
Taiwan	28	7	29	47	22	39	43	46
Thailand	40	17	19	30	13	21	41	53
Industrialized countries	6	3	40	35	30	23	54	62
Japan	13	3	45	41	34	30	42	56
United States	4	2	38	31	29	20	58	67

NOTE: a. Includes mining, manufacturing, construction, power, water supply, and gas.
SOURCES: World Bank. *World Development Report.* New York: WB; Taiwan, Council for Economic Planning and Development. *Taiwan Statistical Data Book.* Taipei: CEPD.

1965 to 19.1 percent in 1987. A global relocation of industrial production capacities towards the Western Pacific is progressing at a rapid pace.

Expansion of exports naturally leads to increased import capacities. The share of the nine countries in world imports increased from 8.5 percent in 1965 to 14.4 percent in 1987. Thus, the region is playing a leading role in sustaining the world economy from the demand side. The Western Pacific countries are gaining a firmer presence in the world economy both in terms of exports and imports.

Asia has long been characterized by its polarized dual structure with Japan, the sole industrial power, as the "center" and other poor countries surrounding it as "peripheries." However, such a structure has clearly started to change due to the strengthened export competitiveness of the developing Asian countries. The gulf that once existed between Japan and the Asian NIEs and ASEAN countries is no longer insurmountable. The Western Pacific region now appears to be in the process of forming a unique economic sphere in which more advanced countries are closely followed by less advanced countries, with "continuous" and moderate gradations in the level of industrial development. In contrast, the relationship between the United States and Latin America, and more so between the EC and Africa, is "discontinuous" with greatly varied levels of development. Their relationship is genuinely in the context of North-South relations. This is not the case for the relationship between Japan and the Asian countries where there is a

Table 12.2

Trade Shares of NIE, ASEAN, Japan and the United States (percentage)

NAME OF COUNTRY/ COUNTRY GROUP	1965	1970	1975	1980	1985	1986	1987
Exports							
NIES[a]	1.6	2.2	2.6	4.0	6.2	6.5	7.4
ASEAN[b]	1.9	1.6	1.9	2.5	2.5	2.1	2.1
Japan	4.9	6.6	6.7	6.8	9.7	10.4	9.6
United States	15.8	14.8	13.1	11.5	11.7	10.7	10.4
Imports							
NIES[a]	2.1	2.9	3.3	4.5	5.6	5.6	6.4
ASEAN[b]	1.9	1.6	1.8	2.0	1.9	1.7	1.8
Japan	4.5	6.2	6.9	7.2	6.8	6.1	6.2
United States	12.7	14.0	12.5	13.1	18.9	18.5	17.3

NOTES: a. Includes South Korea, Taiwan, Hong Kong, and Singapore.

b. Includes Thailand, Malaysia, Indonesia, and the Philippines.

SOURCE: United Nations. *Yearbook of International Trade Statistics.* New York: UN.

"multilayer chasing structure" in which Japan is being caught up by the NIEs and the NIEs are, in turn, being caught up by the less industrialized ASEAN countries.

The level of industrial technology of a country is typically reflected in the level of its machinery industries. In Figure 12.1, which shows the international competitiveness of machinery industries, the ASEAN countries are shown on the left, Japan is shown on the right, and the Asian NIEs are shown in the middle. In other words, the countries are arranged from left to right in accordance with the level of development. The figure clearly shows that the NIEs are rapidly closing the gap in international competitiveness with Japan and, furthermore, the ASEAN countries are quickly catching up with the NIEs. The closing of the gap on the NIEs by the ASEAN countries should be noted as a remarkable phenomenon of recent years.

Let us now consider South Korea as a representative country of the NIEs and Thailand as a representative country of the ASEAN countries. Figure 12.2 shows changes in international competitiveness of major export items of South Korea and Thailand for the period between 1970 and 1985. Items are arranged from left to right in accordance with the level of value added. Items listed on the left of the figure are those with lower value-added per capita and items on the right are those with higher value-added per capita. Clearly, South Korea has succeeded in making its structure of international competitiveness highly sophisticated by becoming less competitive in lower value-added items and by gaining competitiveness very rapidly in higher

Figure 12.1 MULTILAYER CHASING PATTERN OF ASIAN COUNTRIES IN INTERNATIONAL COMPETITIVENESS OF MACHINERY INDUSTRIES

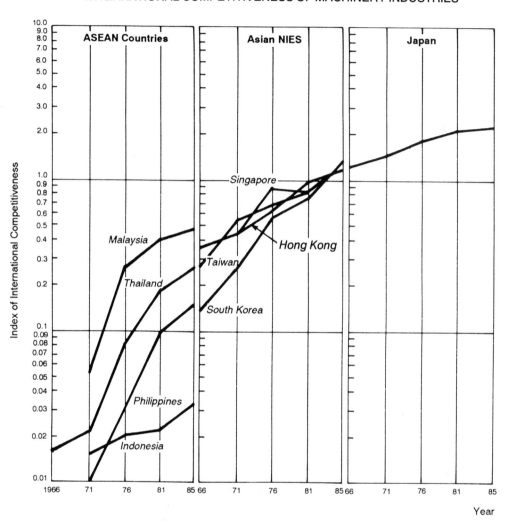

NOTE : International competitiveness of product i of country h is defined as $(E_i^h - E^h)/(W_i - W)$, where E_i^h stands for total export of the product i from country h, W_i for world total exports of the product i, and W for total world exports. When this index exceeds 1.00, the competitiveness of the product i of the country h is above the world average. When the index is below 1.00, it is less competitive than the world average.

SOURCE : United Nations. *Yearbook of International Trade Statistics.* New York: UN.

Figure 12.2 STRUCTURE OF INTERNATIONAL COMPETITIVENESS OF THE NIEs AND ASEAN COUNTRIES, 1970–1985

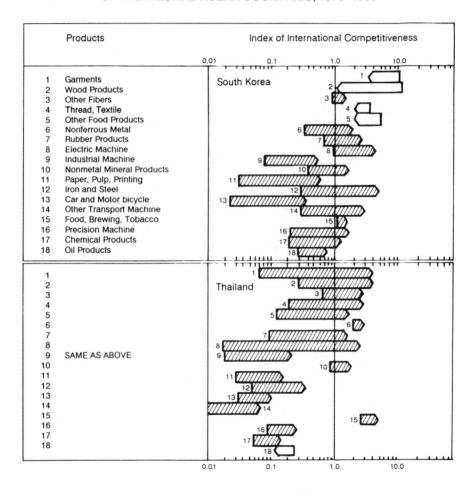

	Products	Index of International Competitiveness
1	Garments	
2	Wood Products	
3	Other Fibers	
4	Thread, Textile	
5	Other Food Products	
6	Nonferrous Metal	
7	Rubber Products	
8	Electric Machine	
9	Industrial Machine	
10	Nonmetal Mineral Products	
11	Paper, Pulp, Printing	
12	Iron and Steel	
13	Car and Motor bicycle	
14	Other Transport Machine	
15	Food, Brewing, Tobacco	
16	Precision Machine	
17	Chemical Products	
18	Oil Products	

NOTE :   For the definition of the Index of International Competitiveness, see Figure 12.1.

SOURCE :   United Nations. *Yearbook of International Trade Statistics.* New York: UN.

value-added items. In contrast, Thailand is acquiring international competitiveness at a remarkable speed in lower value-added items, for which South Korea is now becoming less competitive. This is a clear example of the ASEAN countries "chasing" the NIEs.

The Western Pacific region is called the growing region due to the fact that the region has been forming a unique economic sphere with its aforementioned multilayer chasing relationship. In this relationship, every country in the region has been chased by another and, therefore, every country has been continuously "forced" to increase its productivity and to upgrade its industrial and export structures. In other words, the economic vigor of these countries is nothing other than the fruit of their response against the challenge from the market environment prevailing in the region.

Growth Mechanism of the Western Pacific

Let us now examine the mechanism of industrial development in this region and see how these countries have managed to raise the level of their industries to the point where they can challenge industries in the advanced countries. This mechanism could be described as a "circular mechanism of growth" (Figure 12.3). In general, the capacity of the developing countries to domestically supply capital goods, such as machinery, is limited. Therefore, in order to carry out investments, these countries have to rely on imports from industrialized countries. Thus, investment progresses and productivity increases through the importation of machinery which "embodies" advanced technology. An increase in productivity, in turn, allows the country to start domestic production of industrial goods, the supply of which has thus far totally depended on importation (import substitution). In the next stage, exportation will start. Finally, an increase in exports will

Figure 12.3 CIRCULAR MECHANISM OF GROWTH FOR EXPORTS AND INVESTMENTS

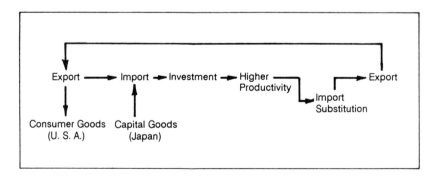

enable further expansion in the importation of capital goods and in investment, and thus will lead to the full functioning of the circular mechanism of
growth. By smoothly exploiting this mechanism, the NIEs and ASEAN
countries were able to accumulate capital and introduce new industrial technology from developed countries. They could be considered as typical success cases in this regard.

Between 1960 and 1986, the share of exports in GDP recorded a remarkable increase in the NIEs and ASEAN countries. It should be noted, however, that the increase in the share of investment has been no less spectacular
(Table 12.3). In recent years, the share of investment in these countries
attained a level that is almost comparable to the average level for industrialized countries. It would be needless to say that the share of imports also
increased dramatically. From the table, we can observe the circular mechanism of growth in which exports and investments are complementing and
reinforcing each other through importation of capital goods embodying
advanced technology.

In this regard, it should be noted that the smooth functioning of the circular mechanism of growth in the NIEs and ASEAN countries required two
indispensable international conditions. The first was the role played by
Japan as an efficient supply base of capital goods. In this sense, Japan could
be called the "supplier" of the economic vigor of the NIEs and ASEAN
countries. In fact, Japanese exports to the NIEs and ASEAN countries have

Table 12.3

Expenditure of Gross Domestic Product in Selected Asia-Pacific Countries
(as a percentage of GDP)

COUNTRY	CONSUMPTION		INVESTMENT		EXPORTS		IMPORTS	
	1960	1986	1960	1986	1960	1986	1960	1986
Hong Kong	94	73	18	23	82	112	94	108
Indonesia	92	76	8	26	13	21	13	23
Malaysia	72	68	14	25	54	57	40	50
Philippines	84	81	16	13	11	25	11	19
Singapore	103	60	11	40	164	123	177	123
South Korea	99	65	11	29	3	41	13	35
Taiwan	87	64	20	17	11	60	18	41
Thailand	86	75	16	21	17	27	19	23
Industrialized countries	78	79	21	21	12	17	11	17
Japan	67	68	33	28	11	12	11	8
United States	81	85	19	18	5	7	5	10

SOURCES: World Bank. *World Development Report*. New York: WB; Taiwan, Council for Economic Planning and Development. *Taiwan Statistical Data Book*. Taipei: CEPD.

greatly exceeded its imports, especially for capital goods for which the excess in exports has been overwhelming.

The second condition was the role played by the United States. With its huge domestic market, the United States has absorbed a large amount of imports from the Asian NIEs and ASEAN countries, thereby enabling these countries to import capital goods from Japan. In this sense, the United States can be called the "absorber" of the economic vigor of the NIEs and ASEAN countries. The trade balance of the United States with the NIEs and ASEAN countries is in deficit for manufactured goods. In contrast, Japan lags far behind the United States in the role of an absorber of exports from the NIEs and ASEAN countries. As shown by the trade balance of the NIEs with the World, Japan, and the United States, for different categories of goods, the NIEs are in deficit with Japan for capital and intermediate goods and in surplus with the United States for consumer goods (Figure 12.4). The trade structure of the NIEs has been to process capital and intermediate goods imported from Japan and export them not to Japan but to the United States.

Indeed, most of the developing countries in the Western Pacific region have succeeded in realizing export-oriented industrialization by strengthening their export capacities through import of capital and intermediate goods from Japan and by exporting to the United States. Without the presence of these two economic giants, Japan and the United States, the circular mechanism of growth and industrialization would not have functioned so smoothly in the Western Pacific.

The difference in the roles of the Japanese and American economies vis-à-vis the developing countries of the Western Pacific region is reflected in the difference in patterns of overseas direct investment of these two countries. American investment in Asian manufacturing industries is characterized by a markedly high ratio of exports to the United States. This tendency is especially noticeable in electrical and electronic industries; domestic sales in these industries account for 12.2 percent of the total sales, while exports to the United States account for 65.2 percent and exports to third countries 22.6 percent. The role of the United States in relation to the developing countries of the Western Pacific region has not been that of a mere absorber of vigor. Through its investment, the United States has created export capacities in Asian countries and then absorbed these exports in its own domestic market. In this sense, the United States has played a very active role.

Japanese direct overseas investments have very different characteristics from those of the United States. The biggest difference lies in the fact that in the case of Japanese investments, the ratio of domestic sales is overwhelmingly high while that of exports is low. Further, the share of exports to Japan is very small and a larger portion of the exports are directed to third coun-

Figure 12.4 NET EXPORTS (EXPORTS–IMPORTS) OF INDUSTRIAL PRODUCTS OF NIEs

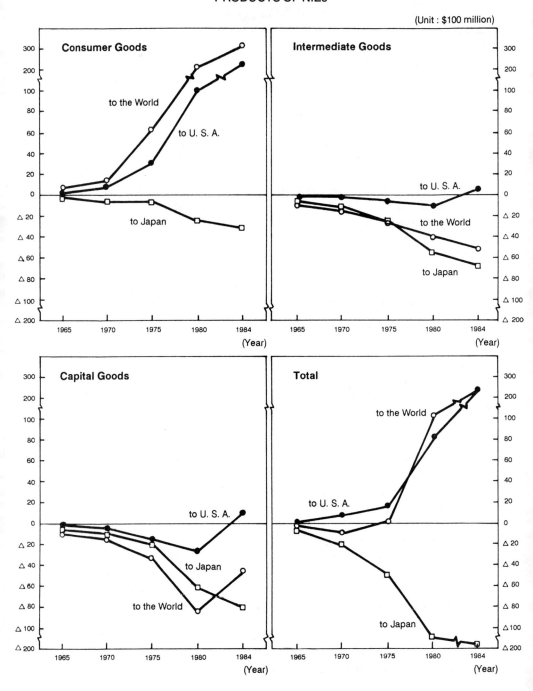

NOTE : △ means "minus".

SOURCE : United Nations. *Yearbook of International Trade Statistics.* New York: UN.

tries. This difference between Japanese and American overseas investments is especially noticeable in electrical and electronic industries. While exports to the United States account for 65.2 percent of the total sales of the overseas American companies in this sector, the corresponding share for overseas Japanese companies is only 21.0 percent. The share of exports to third countries is 22.6 percent for American companies while this share is as high as 41.7 percent for Japanese companies. Clearly Japanese investment strategy has been to pursue exports to third countries, especially to the United States. Thus, although Japan has contributed to the invigoration of the Asian economies, its contribution as an absorber of Asian economic growth has been much less important than that of the United States. This difference in the roles played by the United States and Japan has resulted in the difference in the trade balances of these two countries with respect to the developing countries of the Western Pacific region; there is a big deficit for the former and a big surplus for the latter.

The trade balance of the United States is markedly in deficit not only with the NIEs and ASEAN countries, but also with Japan. In other words, the United States has been acting as a gigantic absorber, engulfing the whole range of merchandise coming from the Western Pacific countries.

The absorber function of the United States was strengthened in a remarkable manner when President Reagan came to power in 1981. The huge fiscal deficit, or the excess in fiscal spending that took place under the Reagan Administration, created demands which were largely in excess of domestic supply capacities. The Western Pacific countries, whose technological levels were rapidly improving during this period, took advantage of American domestic demands and quickly increased their exports. At that time, these countries with increased export capacities were experiencing difficulty in finding market outlets in advanced countries, who were still suffering from the recession after the second oil shock. Thus, these export capacities were directed towards the United States. The share of total exports from Japan destined for the United States increased from 25 percent in 1980 to 37 percent in 1987. Similarly, the share of total exports from the Asian NIEs that was destined for the United States increased from 23 percent to 32 percent over the same period. It is no exaggeration to say that the high economic growth of the Western Pacific countries during the first half of the 1980s was made possible by exports to the United States. The NIEs especially benefited from the fiscal deficit of the United States. From 1981 to 1986, the growth contribution ratio of exports to the United States was as high as 77 percent for Taiwan and 42 percent for South Korea.

Today, however, the United States can no longer endure huge trade deficits with the Western Pacific countries. "Japan bashing" and "NIEs bashing" is intensifying. In the Congress, a rather harsh protectionist movement demanding a mandatory reduction of the trade surplus with particular trade-surplus countries is gaining power. Enactment of such extreme protectionist measures, which may infringe upon the GATT Agreement, has so far been avoided by way of presidential veto. However, frustration seems to be accumulating all the more.

Against the backdrop of such protectionist tendencies in the Congress, the United States government has started to opt for a strengthening of ties with selected countries by way of bilateral free-trade treaties. This change in the American attitude from the defender of multilateral trade principles to the promoter of bilateral trade arrangements is very important, especially in view of the United States' long reign as a staunch defender of GATT principles. The United States concluded a free-trade agreement with Israel in 1985 and signed a similar agreement with Canada in January 1988 (which was effective January 1989). The shadow of a bloc economy, centered around the gigantic economy of the United States, has started to emerge.

At the same time, however, the United States is realizing belatedly that the true reason for trade deficits does not lie in "unfair" practices of trade partners but in the mismanagement of macroeconomic policies. The dramatic fall of stock prices in Autumn 1987 strengthened this perception. "Market forces" convinced people that the American economy cannot sustain a huge trade imbalance for a long period.

Because of the Gramm-Rudman-Hollings Bill, annual fiscal revenues and expenditures should be balanced by 1993. Even though the balance may not be attained in the target year of 1993, it will not be delayed beyond 1995. Together with the move to protectionism and an economic bloc system, efforts to reduce the fiscal deficit have started.

Reduction of the fiscal deficit is an indispensable condition for the health of the American economy and for the stability of the world economy. However, from what has been described, American efforts to reduce its fiscal deficit is nothing less than diminution of its role as a demand-side absorber. The world economy cannot help but be negatively affected by the deflationary effect of a move to reduce the U.S. fiscal deficit. Here lies the serious trade-off that the world economy is now facing. The deflationary effect will affect the Western Pacific countries in particular, whose high growth has been dependent on the growing domestic demand of the United States.

Table 12.4 gives a good example of an attempt to estimate the deflationary impact of a reduction in the American fiscal deficit on the economies of the Western Pacific countries. The table is the result of a policy simulation based on the World Economy Model of the Economics Institute of the Japanese Economic Planning Agency. According to the table, if the fiscal deficit of the United States is reduced by one percent of GNP every year for three consecutive years, the real GNP of the country will be reduced by 1.77 percent

Table 12.4

Economic Impact of a Reduction in the Fiscal Expenditures of
the United States (percentage)

	REAL GNP	REAL DOMESTIC DEMAND	SHORT TERM INTEREST	PRICE	UNEMPLOY- MENT	EXCHANGE RATE	CURRENT ACCOUNT (% TO GNP)
United States							
First year	−1.77	−1.90	−0.64	−0.09	0.77	0.75	0.08
Second year	−3.72	−4.15	−1.45	−0.27	1.49	2.69	0.25
Third year	−5.70	−6.46	−2.69	−0.61	2.26	5.17	0.40
Japan							
First year	−0.32	−0.13	−0.16	−0.11	0.00	−1.11	−0.13
Second year	−1.31	−0.65	−0.40	−0.46	0.02	−3.28	−0.49
Third year	−2.86	−1.54	−0.76	−0.88	0.03	−5.13	−1.04
West Germany							
First year	−0.10	0.04	−0.38	−0.08	0.01	−1.82	0.07
Second year	−0.57	0.04	−0.93	−0.32	0.10	−6.13	−0.02
Third year	−1.57	−0.25	−1.59	−0.64	0.36	−11.38	−0.24
South Korea							
First year	−0.45	−0.25	−0.04	0.19	0.02	–	−0.26
Second year	−2.02	−1.49	−0.64	0.89	0.08	–	−0.72
Third year	−4.54	−3.70	−2.18	1.87	0.17	–	−1.12
World trade							
First year	−0.49						
Second year	−2.08						
Third year	−4.67						

SOURCE: Japan, Economic Institute of the Economic Planning Agency. 1987. *Economic Analysis*, No. III (September).

in the first year, by 3.72 percent in the second year, and by 5.7 percent in the third year; the dollar exchange rate will be devaluated by 0.75 percent in the first year, by 2.69 percent in the second year, and by 5.17 percent in the third year. The decline of domestic demand and the devaluation of the exchange rate will severely affect the South Korean economy which depends substantially on the American economy. The real GNP of South Korea will decline by 0.45 percent in the first year, by 2.02 percent in the second year, and 4.54 percent in the third year, while the current account will deteriorate by 0.26 percent in the first year, 0.72 percent in the second year, and 1.12 percent in the third year. It may come as quite a surprise to many to see how seriously and how rapidly the efforts of the United States to reduce its fiscal deficit will negatively affect the economies of the Western Pacific countries.

The Western Pacific countries are now assuming the role of a spearhead for growth in the world economy. Therefore, keeping these economies vigor-

ous is essential for the healthy growth of the world economy. The future of
the Asian Pacific economies, and that of the world economy, depends on
whether or not a favorable international environment can be created for the
Western Pacific economies. How should Japan and the other Asian countries
react to this enormous task? This issue, the most important issue that the
Western Pacific countries face, is discussed in the next chapter.

CHAPTER THIRTEEN

The Asian Region and Japan

Can Japan be an Engine of Growth for Asia?

The United States is a giant in the Pacific with its huge and diversified domestic market. The Western Pacific countries have been realizing their economic growth by incessantly selling their exports to this gigantic market. The United States has been acting as an eminent "absorber" of the economic vigor of the Western Pacific countries by promoting their economic growth from the demand side. However, as discussed in the previous chapter, favorable conditions for continuous high growth through exports to the United States have been diminishing for the Western Pacific countries. The role to be played by Japan in this area is very important. Japan, with its huge trade surplus, is now expected to replace the United States as a demand-side absorber to mitigate the serious deflationary effect that the reduction in the American fiscal deficit would bring about to the developing countries of the Western Pacific. Japan is expected to protect the world economies from the danger of falling to a lower equilibrium.

In fact, Japan has already started to play this role through the appreciation of the yen. Japanese policies for domestic-demand promotion, such as the Urgent Economic Program, has contributed to the reinforcement of its function as an absorber to some extent. However, it is the high yen that has made the decisive impact. The high yen has increased the real disposable income of Japanese households by stabilizing prices through lower import prices. This, in turn, has stimulated spending by private individuals on household goods and housing. Further, increased household spending, combined with lower import prices of raw materials, parts, and intermediate goods, has induced an increase in capital investments by companies.

In contrast to the strong domestic demand, foreign demand has decreased with lower exports and higher imports. However, the increase in domestic demand has more than offset the decrease in foreign demand, and as a result, 4.5 percent and 5.7 percent of real economic growth was achieved in 1987 and 1988, respectively, despite the appreciation of the yen (Figure 13.1). In the initial stage of the high yen, people were afraid that the super-high yen might deprive the Japanese economy of its vigor, but this fear did not materialize. Instead, the Japanese economy has adapted itself well to the high yen and has even brought about a boom, which could be called "the

Figure 13.1 CONTRIBUTION OF DOMESTIC AND
FOREIGN DEMANDS TO JAPANESE ECONOMIC
GROWTH RATE

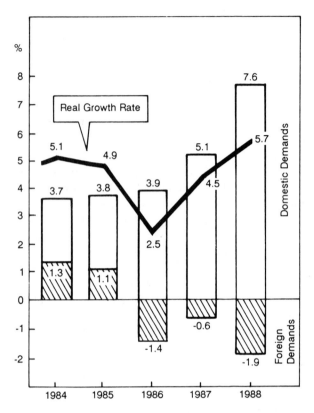

SOURCE :   Japan, Ministry of International Trade and Industry. 1989. *Trade Yearbook*. Tokyo:
             MITI.

high-yen prosperity." The years 1987 and 1988 were memorable ones in
which Japan demonstrated to the world its vigorous ability for self-adjust-
ment, after the adjustment period of 1986.

The increase in Japanese imports has been remarkable, especially imports
of manufactured goods. In 1986 and 1987, imports of manufactured goods
increased at a very high rate of 35 percent and 20 percent, respectively. As a
result, the share of manufactured goods in Japanese imports jumped from
32 percent in 1985 to 44 percent in 1987. A notable increase in the share of
manufactured imports has been recorded for imports from the Asian NIEs
and ASEAN countries. As shown in Table 13.1, the share of manufactured
imports from the Asian NIEs in 1987 was 60 percent and that from the

Table 13.1

Japanese Imports of Manufactured Goods from the NIES and ASEAN[a] (US$ millions)

	TOTAL IMPORTS	TOTAL MANUFACTURED IMPORTS	CHEMICAL PRODUCTS	MACHINERY	OTHER MANUFACTURED GOODS	STEEL	TEXTILES	NONFERROUS METALS	RATIO OF MANUFACTURED IMPORTS TO TOTAL IMPORTS (%)
NIES									
1985	9,838	5,689	498	1,271	3,920	564	1,563	51	57.8
	-2.0	-0.8	-5.1	-1.2	-0.1	-11.3	-8.3	-16.4	
1986	12,519	7,803	759	1,687	5,358	633	2,206	79	62.3
	27.3	37.2	52.4	32.7	36.7	12.2	41.1	54.9	
1987	18,812	12,458	921	2,818	8,719	957	3,594	160	66.2
	50.3	59.7	21.3	67.0	62.7	51.2	62.9	102.5	
ASEAN									
1985	16,719	1,398	155	149	1,093	62	79	597	8.4
	-7.4	-0.4	4.7	-24.0	3.3	34.8	-13.2	-7.3	
1986	13,768	1,483	198	188	1,096	66	97	431	10.8
	-17.7	6.1	27.7	26.2	0.3	6.5	22.8	-27.8	
1987	16,348	2,220	208	244	1,768	131	157	470	13.6
	18.7	49.7	5.0	29.8	61.3	98.5	61.9	9.0	

NOTE: a. Figures in lower rows denote percentage change over previous year.

SOURCE: Japan, Ministry of Finance. *Trade Outlook*. Tokyo: MOF.

ASEAN countries was 50 percent. These figures were distinctly higher than the shares recorded for the EC and the United States, which were 35 percent and 15 percent, respectively. In the past, major Japanese imports from the NIEs were textiles, apparel, and miscellaneous goods, while those from the ASEAN countries were nonferrous metal goods. However, as a result of the high yen and the increased competitiveness of these countries in the export of manufactured industrial goods, the shares of machinery, parts, and intermediate goods in total Japanese imports from these countries have increased considerably. In 1987, machinery imports from the NIEs and ASEAN countries increased by 67 percent and 30 percent, respectively.

This tendency has also been intensified by changes in the behavioral pattern of Japanese exporting companies. The rapid rise in the value of the yen has made it difficult for Japanese exporting companies to produce in Japan and export overseas. Conventional measures against the appreciation of the yen—such as reducing manufacturing costs through rationalization and asking subsidiary suppliers of intermediate goods to accept price reductions—were not effective against the super-high yen. As a result, many companies increased the ratio of overseas procurement for parts and raw materials, and shifted their production bases abroad.

The developing countries of the Western Pacific region were among the prominent hosts of these new production bases of Japanese companies. With this sudden and steep increase, 1987–1988 marked the second turning point for Japanese direct investments in the region (which had commenced in the early 1970s and increased steadily thereafter). In 1986, Japanese direct investment in the Asian NIEs realized an astonishing growth rate of 113 percent and continued to grow by 94 percent in 1987. For the ASEAN countries, Japanese investment stagnated to a certain extent in 1986, due to a decrease in investment in the Philippines. However, in 1987 a high growth rate of 87 percent was recorded over the previous year, mainly due to an increase in investment in Thailand.

The core of Japanese direct investments in Asia is in household electric appliances and other machinery industries. Current patterns of investment are quite different from the past, where investments were made by big companies for assembling and processing of final goods. Parts, intermediate goods, and machinery were imported from Japan and final goods were exported to other countries. Under the new pattern, which is gradually gaining more importance, parts, intermediate goods, and machinery are produced in the Western Pacific region and are exported directly to Japan.

The core of the Japanese machinery industry consists of gigantic assembly companies. These gigantic companies have been characterized by their close ties with affiliated medium- and small-scale companies, from which they purchase various kinds of materials, raw materials, machines, equipment, and parts. This structure of Japanese machine manufacturers contrasts sharply with that of American and European machine manufacturers, which are characterized by vertical integration where supplemental and related production units are kept within their own organizational structures. Therefore, when the rise in the value of the yen pushed Japanese assembly companies towards increased overseas procurement of parts and intermediate goods, and eventually towards overseas production, this change could not help but affect affiliated companies including medium- and small-scale subcontractors. In fact, it was these medium- and small-scale companies that were most seriously affected by the high yen and by the shift of production bases overseas by the big companies. These medium- and small-scale companies responded to the change by shifting their field of business and by starting to move their production bases overseas. If this tendency intensifies, the traditional pattern of "Japanese unity" between large-scale and medium- and small-scale companies will fall apart and the structure of Japanese industries will go through a profound restructuring process that has never been experienced by the country. This process will significantly change the "full-set self-sufficiency type" of the traditional Japanese industrial structure, which has been characterized by the provision of almost all parts, intermediate goods, and machinery equipment by domestic affiliated companies and by very limited induced imports.

The high yen has intensified the role of Japan as a demand-side absorber with Japanese imports of manufactured goods increasingly coming from developing countries of the Western Pacific. Further, the high yen promoted the shift of production bases of Japanese companies overseas and the import of goods from these overseas production bases (out-sourcing). Japanese direct investments have started to play an eminent role in the development of the Western Pacific region by creating export capacities and then by absorbing the outputs of these capacities. In addition to its traditional function of "supply base of capital goods," Japan has strengthened its function as a demand-side absorber for the Western Pacific countries. With these changes, Japan has emerged as a genuine axis of growth in Asia.

Age of Interdependency in Asia

Although Japan has begun to transform itself into a new demand-side absorber for the Western Pacific region, it is not yet certain whether Japan can substitute for the United States. As the rapid expansion of domestic demand during the past two-and-a-half years has proven, the Japanese domestic market has considerable potential. However, it is nevertheless true that the Japanese domestic market is not as large as that of the United States. Moreover, it is unthinkable that Japan will maintain its trade surplus at a level that is sufficiently high enough to keep playing the role of an absorber for the long term. It would be more rational to predict that, if imports continue to grow at the current rate, the Japanese trade balance will turn to deficit in the 1990s.

In the meantime, the economies of the developing countries in the Western Pacific region have kept growing at a very high rate. As a result, their levels of income have risen and the scale of their domestic markets has enlarged considerably. We have to be aware of the fact that developing countries in the Western Pacific region have reached a stage where they can mutually absorb their products. In addition, China, with its huge demand potential and armed with the new strategy of coastal area economic development, has started to emerge in the economic scene of the Western Pacific region. Thus, the dichotomous notion of the region—namely, a region consisting of developed Japan and developing Asia—has become obsolete.

Among the different groups of countries in the Western Pacific, a strong complementary relationship, as well as a competitive relationship, is steadily being formed. In the past, the pattern of the division of labor in the Western Pacific centered around Japan. "Japan versus the Asian NIEs" and "Japan versus the ASEAN countries" dominated country relationships in the region. Today, the relationship among the NIEs and the relationship between the NIEs and the ASEAN countries have gained importance. Further, the relationship between these countries and China can no longer be neglected. We have truly entered into a new era, where the division of labor among the countries in the region has a diversified and multilayered structure.

A dichotomous view of Asia, which divides the region into the North and the South, has often prevented people from seeing an important fact: there is now a highly intensified trade relationship among the NIEs and between the NIEs and ASEAN countries (Table 13.2). In 1987, exports to Japan as a share of the total exports of the Asian NIEs stood at 11.5 percent, while the shares of NIEs exports to the other NIEs and the ASEAN countries were 9.5

Table 13.2

Regional Structure of Exports from Developing Countries of
the Western Pacific, 1987 (as a percentage of total exports to the world)

	JAPAN	NIES	ASEAN	CHINA	UNITED STATES	EC	OTHERS	TOTAL
NIES	11.5	9.5	6.2	6.8	35.1	13.9	17.0	100.0
ASEAN	25.8	20.7	4.0	2.0	20.3	14.2	13.0	100.0
China	16.8	38.2	2.5	–	7.7	9.8	25.0	100.0

SOURCE: United Nations. *Yearbook of International Trade Statistics.* New York: UN.

percent and 6.2 percent, respectively. The total of the latter two groups exceeds the share of exports to Japan. Similarly, exports to Japan as a share of total exports of the ASEAN countries stood at 25.8 percent, while the shares of ASEAN exports to the NIEs and the other ASEAN countries were 20.7 percent and 4.0 percent, respectively. The total of the two groups of countries almost equals the share of exports to Japan. It should therefore be noted that for the NIEs and ASEAN countries, the weight of trade within each group and between the groups has become quite important. For China, the presence of Hong Kong is particularly important. This is reflected in the large share of China's exports going to the NIEs, which stood at 38.2 percent. This was more than double the share of exports to Japan, which stood at 16.8 percent. These figures caution us against overestimating the importance of Japan vis-à-vis China.

It should also be noted that most of the increases are the result of increases in only the past few years. The recent growth of trade among the Asian NIES is particularly remarkable. The trade friction between the United States and Japan, and a rise in import prices from Japan as a result of the high yen, were two factors which directly stimulated this growth. However, the most important reason behind the growth of intraregional trade is that the four NIEs have come to possess industrial bases and have become capable of supplying parts, intermediate goods, and machine equipment. Indeed, the NIEs are in fierce competition with each other. However, the formation of wide-ranging industrial production bases has resulted in the sudden development of a horizontal and complementary relationship among these countries.

The complementary relationship between these countries has been further strengthened by mutual direct investments, which are now actively pursued by the Western Pacific countries. Deceived by the traditional view of the North-South dichotomy, one tends to imagine that direct investments in Asia are monopolized by the two economic superpowers of the region, the United States and Japan. While it is true that the amount of direct investments from these two countries is large, investments of the Asian NIEs in the less developed Western Pacific countries are growing rapidly. The NIEs are expected to become a major source of investment in the ASEAN countries and China in the near future.

Because of their huge trade surpluses with the United States, Taiwan and South Korea have been urged by the United States to adjust their exchange rates. These adjustments are considerable, although they are smaller than the adjustment of the Japanese yen. However, the United States is strongly requesting further appreciation of the New Taiwanese dollar and the won and it will be difficult for Taiwan and South Korea to resist this request. Further adjustment of their currencies will be inevitable. Besides, as a result of their fast economic growth which has lasted for a long time, both Taiwan and South Korea are now experiencing the intensification of labor supply constraints and the steady rise in wages in the industrial sector. In the case of South Korea, repeated labor disputes since the summer of 1987 have further accelerated the rise in wages. Appreciation of currencies and a rise in wages have induced overseas investments of Taiwanese and South Korean enterprises. Enterprises of these two countries seem to be well-prepared for overseas investments, with increases and improvements in their managerial resources during the period of high economic growth and an abundance of experience in foreign transactions that was acquired during the long process of export-oriented industrialization.

In the face of the diminishing demand-side absorbing capacity of the United States, diversification of market outlets has become imperative for the Asian NIEs. The intensification of trade and investment ties among the NIEs and between the NIEs and ASEAN countries is one of the most important elements in this diversification process.

Formation of a Zone of Horizontal Division of Labor in Asia

If the observation made so far is correct, we can expect that in the near future the Western Pacific region will be transformed into a market with an organic internal linkage. In this market, Japan and the other Asian countries will expand mutual importation of industrial goods and mutual direct investment.

As seen in the example of the EC, the key industry for the strengthening of a regional market is the machinery industry. The machinery industry is characterized by a very broad range of division of labor, as it includes manufacturing of innumerable kinds of parts and intermediate goods. No other industry can provide a broader range of the "division of labor between different steps of the manufacturing process." Through this mechanism, the machinery industry allows countries to specialize in different steps for which they have comparative advantages. In each of the EC member countries, for example, the machinery industry has the largest share of exports and also retains the largest share of imports. This demonstrates that a country cannot be self-sufficient in the machinery industry, which requires the production of a variety of parts and intermediate goods. Instead, development of a country inevitably leads to expansion of imports at the same time that there is expansion of exports.

Because of these characteristics, the machinery industry permits a country to develop both exports and imports with its trade partners within the same category of industry. This is called a horizontal division of labor. In this context, when we look at the export expansion of the Asian NIEs, the high export ratio of machinery should be noted (electrical and electronic machinery, transportation machinery, precision machinery, and general machinery).

In 1987, the export ratio of machinery stood at 38 percent in Singapore, 33 percent in South Korea, 31 percent in Taiwan, and 21 percent in Hong Kong. They are rapidly narrowing the gap with developed countries, whose average export ratio of machinery was 42 percent.

Following the Asian NIEs, the ASEAN counties are strengthening their competitiveness in machinery exports. Combined with active investments of Japanese machinery manufacturing companies in the region, this will substantively contribute to the transformation of the Western Pacific region into a zone of horizontal division of labor.

The development of a horizontal division of labor will certainly have a strong impact on the traditional industrial structure of Japan. Japan has long been characterized by what I call a "full-set, self-sufficiency type" of industrial structure, in which a full set of machinery, ranging from consumer goods to parts, intermediate goods, and manufacturing machinery, is produced locally. Because of this structure, the expansion of the domestic economy or of exports induced only a limited increase in imports; this partly explains the surplus in Japan's trade balance. Industrial development of the Asian NIEs and ASEAN countries, accompanied by the high yen, provides a good opportunity for a change in the Japanese full-set, self-sufficient industrial structure. Such a structure has become obsolete in view of the large size of the Japanese economy and its impact on the world. The progress of the horizontal division of labor between Japan and the Asian counties will force Japan to carry out structural adjustments and these structural adjustments in Japan will further accelerate the process of horizontal division of labor. We must take full advantage of the "mutual-strengthening mechanism" between a horizontal division of labor and structural adjustment.

The Japanese tend to regard the rapid modernization and expansion of exports of South Korea and the Asian NIES as a "catching up" of these Asian developing countries and take a defensive position. This reaction is understandable since Japan, which has been busy "chasing" advanced European and American countries, has never had the experience of being chased. However, the size of the present Japanese economy is too large to permit such a defensive posture, and the Japanese should be more positive in accepting the growing horizontal division of labor in the region.

The economic strengthening of its neighboring countries offers Japan the possibility of developing a sophisticated and horizontally complementary relationship with these countries. This relationship will then create dynamic mutual economic effects among these countries. I would like to conclude this book by stating that whether or not Japan can build a new economic system that permits a harmonious development of the world economy depends heavily on the way Japan reacts to the new waves of development in the Asian countries.

INDEX

171